The Gates of the Kingdom Book Series

The Gates of the Kingdom

Part 3

by Colin Russell Baker

Published by Kingdomgates Publishing in the Northern Territory of Australia.
www.kingdomgatespublishing.com.au
Copyright © 2012 Colin Baker. All rights reserved. No portion of this book may be reproduced, stored in a retrieval system, or transmitted in any form or by any means – electronic, mechanical, photocopy, recording, scanning, or other – except for brief quotations, without prior written permission of the publisher.

ISBN 10: 1922223999

ISBN 13: 978-1-922223-99-9

Published in Australia

Dedicated to the Great King, our glorious Lord and Savior, Yeshua the Messiah; Adonai Kabod; the Lord of Glory.

✽ ✽ ✽ ✽ ✽

Contents

Hadad-Rimmon to Kiryat-Arba; a Land of Giants and Kings

Part 1 15

Part 2 21

Death; the Terrible Gate 33

The Jordan Gate 43

The Jordan Gate II 47

The River Gate & The Canal Gate . . . 53

The Fire Gate Part 1 55

The Fire Gate Part 2 69

The Gate in Session 83

The Little Gate of the Great King

Part 1 89

Part 2 103

Part 3 129

Part 4 149

The Jordan Gate III 161

Contents (Continued)

The Communion Gate . . . , ... 173

The Tzion Gate 179

Other Books by Colin Baker 187

Other Copyright. 189

About the Author 191

'The Gates of the Kingdom' is a book series which will take you on a spiritual pilgrimage, exploring events where the realms of Heaven and Earth have touched.

This pilgrimage is through places which will often be foreign to you. The names of people, places, and relationship terms have been preserved in their original language so that you will get a sense of the cross-cultural context of this amazing story.

You will notice that the narrator speaks only in English, and that his paragraphs always appear indented for your convenience.

Some of the characters are a bit rough around the edges, and some speak with strange accents. These are not spelling mistakes. It will be well worth the effort of getting used to 'reading what you see' with these fellas.

A line dividing text indicates a switching of realms.

The Heritage Series consists of four parts…

The Gates of the Kingdom

~

A story of seed-time and harvest, of sprouting and blossoming, of bearing fruit with seed unto the fullness ... A Kingdom sown, a Kingdom reaped, a glorious Bride without spot or wrinkle, a matchless gift from a Father to a Son; bone of His bone and flesh of His flesh.

Heritage Series

Part 3:

Paw-Rach! The Rod Buds!

Prologue:

There is a river whose streams gladden the city of God, the holy habitation of 'Elyon. (Psalm 46:4 CJB)

...And in the darkness, the roar of rushing waters; the upper Jordan ... Between the ridge and the thicket; a fire, and twelve men. They have much to talk about; very much, for they have come such a long way ...a way they had never walked before ...

"Mmm! Oh, that'sho goodg!" says Igal with a mouth full of hot fish.

"Yeah, you're not wrong, but to buy fish with the gold of Misrayim!?"[1]

"Don't blame me. It was Shamua's idea. He talked me into it."

"Well, he didn't have to try very hard, did he?" Laughter redounding around the fire…

"Oh, it's really good," says Gadiel, wiping his mouth on the sleeve of his jacket, "but even so, the story of twelve strangers who buy fish with a gold ring will be all over the village tonight. We all know what that means."

"It means we won't be sleeping by a fire tonight." answers Joshua, "That's what it means!"

"We'll sleep in a den under that ridge, the rain's coming back again anyway." states Caleb with typical disinterest in junior opinion.

The roaring of lions fighting over some morsel, which had been going on since sunset, suddenly catches everyone's attention. They all turn toward the blackness of the ridge.

"Oh don't worry about that. They're only beasts," says Caleb, "We'll soon chase them away. At least

---

1   Misrayim: Two Kingdoms; Egypt

we won't have to worry about the locals prowling on the scent of Gibtan[2] gold."

"No; only the local mosquito's prowling on the scent of fresh meat!" contributes Joshua.

"There are more than mosquito's that are hungry for fresh meat around here." confesses Palti of Zebulun, "It's a wonder any of us survived Kivrot-HaTa'avah[3]."

"Eloheinu[4] is not a man Palti," interjects the ever silent Sethur, son of Michael of Asher, "no flesh can stand before him. He is the only true Elohim[5]."

"Yes, that's true. And right there our faith shall be tested before this journey is over my 'ah." warned Joshua as he stood to turn his jacket which was drying by the fire.

"What about Moshe," questioned Gadiel, "doesn't he stand before Y'haveh?"

All eyes turn towards Sethur expecting him to concede, but it was Joshua who had the answer.

"No. It is Y'haveh himself who brings my lord Moshe and places him before his face. It is by his sovereign grace that Moshe stands before him, and

---

2   Gibtan: of Gibt (Gibt being the ancient language of Egypt.)
3   Kivrot-HaTa'avah: The Graves of Lust
4   Eloheinu: Our God
5   Elohim: Great One (plural); God

it is by his sovereign grace that any of us survived Kivrot-HaTa'avah."

Shaphat of Simeon passes his remaining fish on to Shamua of Reuben: "The fish is so-so. I can take it or leave it," he says, swallowing hard.

Some light-hearted disbelief echoes around the fire at Shamua's feigned piety, but Joshua picks up on it…

"Shamua is right, we should not presume upon the grace of Y'haveh. Tomorrow we shall split up into two's. A group of twelve aliens shall not be seen moving south from here. We'll meet by the waters of Meram, outside the fortress of Hatzor; east of Kedesh. From there we'll go up into the hill country and spy out the land to the west and the south."

"What about the Tzidonim[6]? Wouldn't it be risky to go to the west?"

"No, we'll not go near the coast. We'll turn south and down the west of Tavor across the great plain by Hadad-Rimmon. The stories of the richness of that valley are known throughout the earth. We shall see if the stories are true and find out what manner of people live in such a place."

---

6   Tzidonim: Sidonians

"I hope they're not like the Refa'im[7]." says Gadiel with an ominous tone.

"No my 'ah, don't worry," replies Joshua, "They are not like the Refa'im. The giants live in the forests and the hills. They don't have the numbers to hold the plain, but they might raid it. The people of the plain will be very numerous. They'd have to be trading with the Tzidonim. This is what Moshe told me that he'd heard of in Misrayim."

"Bashan; the land of the Refa'im is wild country. It lies to the east beyond that ridge and south as far as the 'Avarim Ranges. The Refa'im know only one law; 'winner takes all'!"

"'Thundering Pomegranate!'" exclaims Igal, deliberately changing the subject, "I wonder what sort of place would bear a name like that?"

"'Hadad-Rimmon;' no… I've never heard of anything like it," says Sethur as they all rise to depart. The ever wise Caleb says nothing, but with just the hint of a knowing smile on his face, he snuffs the fire with leftover fish, the aroma wafting up into the night air.

❈ ❈ ❈ ❈ ❈

---

7   Refa'im: Rephaim; 'Ghosts of the Dead Ones'; descendants of the Nephtilim; giants.

Hadad-Rimmon to Kiryat-Arba: A Land of Giants and Kings...

Part 1

"It's vast!" gasped Shaphat. "And so green!" exclaimed Palti, as they all stood on the northern crest of the great plain for the first time. It was so far across; they could barely make out the other side.

"Cleared, fertile land … And full of crops!" exclaimed Caleb, "A land flowing with milk and honey. It's true! The stories are true!"

"Look! There are orchards!"

"Yes, and look over there! … Vineyards!"

"There are roads and villages with walls. I count six in this area alone," says the ever vigilant Joshua, "and look over there! What is that?"

"If it's a caravan, then it's the biggest caravan I've ever seen." says Gadiel.

"No my 'ah, it's not a caravan. I think it's a procession of some kind," says Caleb, "I can see banners!"

"Yes, and look; there are others coming out from that vineyard to join them with more banners and they're pulling wagons with casks."

"Must be wine!" says Palti with an all too obvious interest.

"Yes, I agree," confirms Joshua thoughtfully. "I think it could be a celebration of grape harvest. There are so many people in that procession. An extra twelve would never be noticed."

"The road runs straight across the plain. They're going to Hadad-Rimmon, and so are we!"

"Remove your tunics and your swords. Kalev and I shall carry them. You shall be unarmed men on your way to a holiday celebration. We shall be your eved."

They stepped out into the open, hurried down the slope, and at length, joined the procession.

"This is fun!" says Igal, "We should've brought a banner!"

"Keep your mouth shut and your ears open!" shouts 'Ammi'el in an angry whisper.

"Look at all those beautiful women. They're hardly wearing anything at all!" says Shamua as he collides with a big sack of fruit on a pole slung across the shoulders of one enormous slave.

The slave turns and frowns him something awful, but does nothing.

"Did you see his hands and feet 'ah?" asks an amazed Nachbi.

"Yeah!" replies Gadiel, "No thumbs, no big toes! That's cruel!"

"Shamua … That wagon of women; they're temple prostitutes! I think this is not just a harvest festival," says Sethur. "I don't like the looks of this at all."

A rumbling sound in the distance catches every ones attention, and the whole procession turns to look.

Immediately a word starts reverberating through the crowd; 'Observant!' 'Observant!' 'Yabin!' 'Yabin!' The whole procession comes to a halt as wagons, carts, bulls and donkeys are turned aside. Everyone scrambles to get off the road…

"Who is it?" asks the younger 'servant' of the older.

"It's Yavin, king of Hatzor!" replies Caleb…

"Quick! Get behind that wagon!" commands Joshua in a whisper. "Let's pray that he's not what his name suggests."

"Hatzor is the biggest fortress we've seen yet. The citadel itself is enormous. It's the seat of power for this whole region. This, will be very interesting."

The thunder of a hundred horses and the unmistakable clatter of armor came upon us just as the last child was snatched from the road. The massive chariot of Yavin came first with shield-bearers riding alongside. It was drawn by a team of ten horses. Yavin was reclining on his couch with women and wine.

He paid us no attention at all, but the people all bowed down. There was obvious fear in the air.

We watched through the railing of the wagon. The king's chariot was followed by a dozen more with very big men riding in them, heavily armed ... The king's bodyguard.

As each chariot passed by, all eyes turned toward us, but none saw us. We had hidden behind the wagon of the temple prostitutes. We were all covered in dust. The women were baring their breasts to the passing soldiers, who were making lewd gestures back at them and calling out obscenities.

Our worst enemy, 'Observant' had just passed by within a few cuvits of us and never even knew we were there.

It was then that Y'hoshua said something to me that I've never forgotten.

"Kalev," he said, "nothing is so blinding to a man as lust. My 'ah, we must guard our eyes!"

"We shall not enter the city. For the sake of our 'ah, Shamua, we shall surely not go in."

"Once we've seen the wall and the gates, we'll camp in the fields overnight. In the morning, we'll turn south towards Sh'khem and Y'vus."

That night the stars came out and a stillness settled over the fields. There was a most comforting calm in the air. Even the noise of the city could not disturb our peace. We felt the presence of Y'haveh very close. We worshiped and we slept.

❊ ❊ ❊ ❊ ❊

The Gates of the Kingdom

~

A story of seed-time and harvest, of sprouting and blossoming, of bearing fruit with seed unto the fullness ... A Kingdom sown, a Kingdom reaped, a glorious Bride without spot or wrinkle, a matchless gift from a Father to a Son; bone of His bone and flesh of His flesh.

Heritage Series

Hadad-Rimmon to Kiryat-Arba: A Land of Giants and Kings

Part 2

We started out at first light, and by sunset we had reached Mount 'Eival. We slept in the open country to the north of the mountain because we'd been warned about bandits.

Very early the next morning, we moved quietly through the rubble of 'Eival and out into the sunshine of the most beautiful little valley one could ever imagine.

There, nestled between the two mountains of G'rizim and 'Eival, was the citadel of Sh'khem. It had a great tower which rose far above the wall.

When our 'av, Ya'akov was living there, he purchased land from Hamor, the Hivi, ruler of Sh'khem. He dug a well and built an altar to El-Elohei-Yisra'el[8]. At that time, Shim'on and Levi killed all the men of Sh'khem in reprisal for our sister Dinah. *(...these teachers are zealous for you, but their motives are not good. Galatians 4:17)* *(What has been will be.)*

It seems that since then, Sh'khem has been occupied by the P'lishtim, who worship the Ba'alim. This was obvious to us by the huge fertility pole (felic symbol) to their goddess ashera which was by the great oak outside the city gate. People wishing to enter were required to kiss it.

Again, we turned aside and did not enter.

As we approached G'rizim on the road south, we could see a small village and a market. It was the well of Ya'akov. As soon as we saw it, we all became very thirsty. We emptied our water bags onto the ground and made a bee-line for that well.

When we realized how deep it was (about 75 cuvits), we had to ask one of the local women, who had a rope and bucket, to draw water for us.

---

8   El-Elohei-Yisra'el: God, the God of Israel.

...but whoever drinks the water I will give him will never be thirsty again! On the contrary, the water I will give to him will become a spring of water inside him, welling up into eternal life. (John 4:14 JNT)

This was our own water and our own land. We had come home!

Efrayim and M'nasheh hugged each other as tears rolled down the cheeks of Y'hoshua and Gadi. The locals looked on in bewilderment at these two brothers crying with uncontrollable joy.

This would be the resting place for the bones of their 'av Yosef, which we had carried on oath all the way from Misrayim.

The highway from Sh'khem to Beit-El was a busy road. We saw many teams of oxen pulling heavy loads and slaves under the whip of cruel men. Misrayim lunged into our faces again! There were soldiers everywhere. We later discovered them to be a detachment sent by Adonai-Tzedek, king of Y'vus, for the building of Beit-El. We followed the road from the crest of the eastern hill.

As we passed by Beit-El, we could see that the wall and the gates were already complete, and that all the burdens of 'Misrayim' and the highway were pouring into the city through an open gate. We were shocked to see the 'House of God' a foreign house in a slave state, and we wondered at the name of the king of Y'vus; 'My Lord is Righteousness'!?

While we were still in sight of that city, we came to a hill between Beit-El and Ai, to the place where Y'haveh had appeared to our 'av, Ya'akov. It was here on this hill that he, like Avraham had done before him, built an altar. It was here that he saw angels descending and ascending on one, like a ladder, joining heaven and earth. This was the true Beit-El! We were awed by the sacredness of that place! It was far outside the city gate.

The distance from Beit-El to Y'vus was not far, but there were even more soldiers on that road. We waited on a hilltop for more than half a day, looking for a way to travel the road without being noticed by the soldiers.

Eventually we spotted a caravan of Midyanim merchants carrying opium into the affluent city of Y'vus. We followed closely behind our estranged brothers; close enough to talk with their children…

"Is that your dogie?" The boy clutches the pup close to his breast and frowns.

"Oh; sorry! My name is Palti. What's your name?"

"My name is 'Onam. I am ben Nassi' 'Adna (the son of prince 'Adna) and this is my dog. His name is H'dwah. We are going to Y'bus."

"Do you come here often?"

"Yes, my 'arba[9] is a friend of the king and my doda is a guest in the royal palace. We are the only ones allowed to bring opium for the king. We come often. One time the king even sent his soldiers to protect us!"

"Oh, it's a great honor to walk with such esteemed company. My brothers and I are also traveling to Y'vus, but unlike you, my honored 'ah, we have never been there before. We shall probably get lost in the city."

The boy looks at Palti with an expression of disbelief on his face: "Only the Y'busi and Emori are allowed into the citadel. You and your brothers had better follow us or you'll end up losing your heads! The king doesn't like strangers!"

"What's he like; the king?"

"He's as big as that wagon over there, and his sword is long enough to go through six men at once! He has never been defeated in battle! No king of the Y'vusi ever has! My 'arba says; 'never trust them, and never treat them with contempt!'"

"My little 'ah; it sounds like your "arva' is a very wise man."

---

9   'arba: Amorite & Midianite name for father. 'av (Hebrew); 'ab (ancient Hebrew); abba (Greek)

"Yes. And it's just as well you introduced yourself Palti, because he also says that I should never talk to strangers!"

"'Onam, my name is Y'hoshua; we would be honored to speak with your 'arba. When you see him next, please tell him that we are here and that we wish to speak with him."

Immediately, the boy ran on ahead. A short time later, he re-appeared on the hind of a donkey, riding behind a man of obvious substance. The rider turned in beside us and spoke; "I am 'Adna, my son tells me that you wish to speak with me."

"Yes. Shalom! I am Y'hoshua. We, your eved, returning from a long journey, are in need of rest and supplies. Would you be so gracious as to advise your eved the correct way to enter Y'vus; to the market place? We are your 'ah, but we're not familiar with this city."

"If you enter this city, you will never get out alive. If you think you can come with me, I will turn you in at the city gate. You in fact are my 'ah; you are sons of Yitz'chak! You are spies and if I so much as whistle, you will all be dead men!"

"All of Canaan is in dread of you. We have heard what your God did to the Gibtans. Adonai Tzedek has put a price on your heads just on the expectation that you will be coming!"

"We are greatly indebted to you 'ahi for your warning."

"It was your God who caused you to meet me and not someone else. Adonai Tzedek is holding my 'ahot to guarantee delivery of his opium. She is young. She has no breasts."

"How can we capture Y'vus?"

"It cannot be done. Only an elohim who drowns the armies of Gibt could do that!"

"Is it possible to reach the road south to Kiryat-Arba[10] without going through the city?"

"Yes, but you should go at night, because soldiers patrol the Gichon valley during the day. They're afraid to enter it at night. There's a road by the olive grove on the far side of the wadi. It turns up into the valley of the Refa'im, then runs south to Kiryat-Arba."

"Thank you 'ahi, may the blessings of the God of Avraham, Yitz'chak and Ya'akov rest upon you, and may the power of El-Shaddai shelter your 'ahot!"

We stopped and shared a meal together near the place where we left the road. As the shadows lengthened, we parted company with much goodwill.

---

10 Kiryat-Arba: The City of Arba' or literally; the city that father built; built by Arba, the tallest of the giants; Hebron

"Shalom[11], 'ahi!"

"Shalom! Shalom! …Shalom aleikhem[12]!"

As we came near the walls of Y'vus, peace gave way to a very real sense of danger and, true to the word of Nasi' 'Adna, the soldiers all retreated from the approaching darkness … One even saw us, but was in too much of a hurry to stop.

As far as we could make out, Y'vus was an impenetrable fortress with massive walls on top of a mountain. If not for the encouragement of our friend, our despair would have been deeper than one could imagine.

We walked cautiously through the narrow plain of the Refa'im by night. The first hour brought us to a wadi that smelt like a refuse dump. On closer inspection, it turned out to be some sort of open grave. The remains we saw in the dim light of the fire-sticks looked as though they had been butchered and cooked. We snuffed out the torches and moved on, stopping often at any sound of man. The morning found us approaching a fork in the road. Now what would we do? None of us knew which way to turn but Y'hoshua was looking for a sign.

---

11 Shalom: peace, tranquility, safety, wellbeing, contentment, success

12 Shalom aleikhem: peace be upon you all

"Somewhere not far from here we'll find the standing stone of the grave of our 'em, Rah'el. It's beside the road to Hevron."

True to the word of Y'hoshua, we found the standing stone of Rah'el's grave a short distance along the upper road.

When we saw it, Palti began to weep. Y'hoshua and Gadi joined him. We were all deeply touched by a sense of homecoming, of finding our roots in the land.

We continued south through the valley of Eshkol. It was full of ripe fruit. Grapes and pomegranates were plentiful and many other fruits besides. We decided to come back later to gather samples for our brothers. Hevron would be our last stop before returning to the camp in Pa'ran.

When we finally reached Kiryat-Arba, that is Hevron, we sat and watched the gate of the city for two days.

There was much commerce in and out of the gate, mostly P'lishtim from the coastal regions of Gath and Gaza. There were also B'douvin and Edomi traders who approached from the south.

The strangest thing we noticed was that they never closed the gate. Not even at night. The guards on the gate seemed to be only interested in enforcing the gate tax.

We discovered that the king was very rich and it's no wonder. He charged us half a shekel of silver each just to enter the city! It seemed that a foreign army would have been welcome, providing they all paid their gate tax!

We also noticed that soldiers from Y'vus came and went as they wished without stopping at the gate. The Emori and the Y'vusi were still brothers and still good friends. This was not good news for us. Some of my brothers began to voice their discouragement, but Y'hoshua and I kept our peace.

While we were in the market, on the street between the city gate and the palace gate, a great chariot rolled in behind a team of six horses. We thought it strange because the driver could barely see over the cowling, so I remarked to the fruit merchant I was dealing with; "A little big for the driver is it not?"

The man grinned; "You are a stranger to this city, no? Ha! You wait and see when it comes back out that gate. Ha! Ha ha ha!"

I felt embarrassed that I didn't understand the joke. Obviously the man knew something that I didn't. We waited.

We almost feinted when the gate swung open and that chariot came through. The driver was so big that he had to duck as he went through the gate!

Our friend, the fruit merchant, laughed so hysterically when he saw our faces that everyone turned to see who he was laughing at. Even the giant in the chariot turned and gave us the most hideous grin.

"Who is that?!!" I asked in utter disbelief at his size.

"That, is Achiman; the champion of the king's guard. He has two brothers and they are even bigger than he is! Ha! Ha! Ha ha ha. Forgive me my friend, but your faces … it is the same with all who see the sons of Anak for the first time. Ha! Ha ha ha."

"Now you know the meaning of the saying; 'Who can stand against the sons of Anak!' Don't stare at his brothers when you see them. They both have very bad tempers. Oh! Hee! He! He! Cough! Cough! Cough!"

We felt about the size of grasshoppers! I looked at S'tur and his face was white, like he'd seen a ghost, his own ghost! The word of Y'hoshua had come true again!

Y'hoshua called me aside: "Did you see all the gaps in his armor? We'll need to train some of our archers to use heavier arrows to deal with these

Anakim. It is they who shall not stand before the armies of Adonai!"

We moved on from Kiryat-Arba, but we had been violently shaken, each man keeping his own council.

After taking fruit from the valley of Eshkol, we travelled as quickly as we could back to Pa'ran, to the tabernacle of Eloheinu and to the thousands of Isra'el. We had been away forty days.

* * * * *

The Gates of the Kingdom

~

A story of seed-time and harvest, of sprouting and blossoming, of bearing fruit with seed unto the fullness ... A Kingdom sown, a Kingdom reaped, a glorious Bride without spot or wrinkle, a matchless gift from a Father to a Son; bone of His bone and flesh of His flesh.

Heritage Series

Death; The Terrible Gate

The bunch of grapes we presented before the sons of Isra'el was so big that it had to be carried on a pole between two of us. We had all taken turns carrying it. It was that heavy!

When we displayed the fruit of the land to the people, we were actually holding up the symbols of life before their eyes. One would have thought that after all this time in the desert, where there was no life, they would have understood the meaning of the sign, but they did not. They saw only food and drink. Life was hidden from their eyes!

Then, as we started giving our report, I suddenly realized that it was only Y'hoshua and myself who knew in our hearts the glory of Adonai!

"...the people living in the land are fierce," they said, "and the cities are fortified and very large. Moreover, we saw the 'Anakim there," they said. 'Amalek lives in the area of the Negev; the Hitti, the Y'vusi, and the Emori live in the hills; and the Kena'ani by the sea and alongside the Yarden."

The people, when they heard this; they were all thrown into a panic.

I silenced them around Moshe and shouted; "We ought to go up immediately and take possession of it; there is no question that we can conquer it."

But the men who had gone with us all made excuses, saying; "We can't attack those people because they are stronger than we are." And; "...the land devours its inhabitants."

"All the people we saw there were giant! We saw the N'filim, the descendants of 'Anak, who was from the N'filim; to ourselves we looked like grasshoppers by comparison, and we looked that way to them too!"

At this, all the people of Isra'el cried out in dismay and wept all night long.

The next day, when Moshe had called the whole assembly into the tent of meeting, they started grumbling, and they said to each other, "…we will die by the sword. Our wives and little ones will be taken as booty! Let's appoint a leader, and return to Egypt!"

Moshe and Aharon fell on their faces before the whole community in the tent. Y'hoshua and I tore our clothes and cried out in utter desperation; "The land we passed through …is an outstandingly good land!"

"If Y'haveh is pleased with us, then he will bring us into this land and give it to us! It's a land flowing with milk and honey! Only don't rebel against Y'haveh. Don't be afraid of the people living in the land. We'll eat them up! Their defense has been taken away from them. Y'haveh is with us!"

But the people wouldn't listen. They began crying out; "Stone them! Stone them!" Fear had so gripped them that they didn't even remember where they were!

Then the glory of Y'haveh appeared in the tabernacle.

Y'haveh said to Moshe; "How long will this people treat me with contempt? How much longer will they not trust me, especially considering all the signs I've performed among them?"

"Surely, as I live, all the earth shall be filled with the glory of Y'haveh, for all the men who are seeing my glory, and my signs which I've done in Egypt and in the wilderness and have tried me these ten times, and have not listened to my voice; they shall not see the land which I have sworn to their fathers. Yea, not one of those scorning me shall see it."

"My 'eved, Kalev, because there's another spirit in him, and he's fully following me, I shall bring him into the land into which he's gone. His seed shall possess it."

"As for you, your lifeless bodies shall fall in this wilderness, even all your numbered ones…from twenty years old and upward, in that you've murmured against me."

"You'll certainly not come into the land which I lifted up my hand to cause you to live in, except for Kalev ben Y'funeh, and Y'hoshua ben Nun."

"As for your infants, of whom you've said, 'they'll be a prey,' I'll bring them in, and they shall know the land which you've rejected, but your carcasses shall fall in this wilderness!"

"By the number of days in which you spied out the land, forty days, a day for a year, you shall bear your iniquities; forty years. You shall know my alienation from you. (You shall know death.) I am Y'haveh; I have spoken!"

And so it was my friend; we wandered about in the wilderness forty years, and we knew death. Y'haveh was with us as before. He continued to speak, to care and to instruct, but we knew death. We knew his alienation. We learnt what it was like to live without life.

Over seven hundred people fell every week for forty years!

A death every day in every clan until that generation had completely passed away. And Y'haveh got glory over the generation that despised him, even as he had done over Par'oh. If it were not for the word of Y'haveh and his presence with us, we'd have all perished.

When we turned back into the wilderness, we grieved and we mourned. Y'haveh moved forward, ever forward … and we followed him. He gave us a ritual; a way to move forward in death, that is, in the wilderness. We didn't know what to do or which way to go, but Y'haveh would tell us, and we would follow.

Lifeless ritual became a way for us to survive his alienation. We knew not where it would take us, but as we died and as we followed, Y'haveh was getting glory in us. We were starting to become strong as a people. Not by the ritual, but simply by trusting and following.

We were also a people under discipline, and we learned our lessons the hard way.

One time, while we were in the desert, we found a man collecting firewood on Shavat. When Moshe and Aharon inquired of Adonai as to what should be done to him, they were told that the whole congregation should take him outside the camp and stone him. And so we did.

Well; the man had obviously forgotten that he was ben Isra'el. Nor did he understand that we were not the same as all the other peoples on the face of the earth. It was actually quite an unearthly thing to stone a man who failed to rest. Many in the camp were quite unable to come to grips with the reality of who we now were.

Y'haveh understood our need, and so he commanded that we sew tassels on our garments with blue threads in them. These were to remind us that we were now the people of Y'haveh; a heavenly people, a holy nation, a kingdom set apart.

Even so, there was still unrest in the camp. It was not long before Korach, one of the seventy, rose up to challenge the leadership of Moshe and Aharon. Two hundred and fifty leaders of the council rose up with him…

"You assume too much authority! The entire congregation; all of them are holy! Y'haveh is among them. Why then do you lift yourselves up above the assembly of Y'haveh?"

Moshe immediately fell on his face, then he spoke to Korach and all his company saying, "In the morning Y'haveh will show who are his and who is holy and who he chooses to come near to him!"

"Do this; take censers for yourselves and put fire in them, and put incense on them before Y'haveh tomorrow, and whoever Y'haveh chooses; he is holy!"

"It is you who assume too much, you sons of Levi!"

Well, to cut a long story short, fire came out from Adonai and consumed the two hundred and fifty elders. As for Korach and his friends, well, the earth opened her mouth at the word of Moshe, and swallowed them up. They went down into the grave screaming!

The very next day the whole community assembled against Moshe and Aharon, saying, 'You have killed the people of Y'haveh!'

The cloud came over the tent of meeting. The glory of Y'haveh appeared. Moshe and Aharon came to the front of the tent and Y'haveh said, 'Get away from this assembly and I will destroy them at once!'

They fell on their faces.

Moshe said to Aharon, 'Hurry, take your fire pan, put fire from the altar in it, lay incense on it, and run to the assembly. Anger has gone out from Y'haveh and the plague has already begun!'

Aharon did as Moshe had said. He ran into the midst of the assembly and stood between the dead and the living, to make atonement for them. The plague was stopped. Over fourteen thousand, people died that day!

Y'haveh said to Moshe, *'Speak to the sons of Israel and take from each of them a rod, for a father's house, from all their rulers, for the house of their fathers, twelve rods. You shall write the name of each on his rod. And you shall write Aaron's name on the tribe of Levi; for one rod shall be for the head of their father's house.'*

And you shall place them in the tabernacle of the congregation, before the testimony where I shall meet with you. And it shall be that the man's rod which I choose shall blossom. And I shall cause the murmurings of the sons of Israel, which they are murmuring against you to cease from Me.'

When Moshe brought out all the rods the next day, he presented them before the eyes of the people. Aharon's rod had budded, blossomed, and even born ripe almonds! The proof was in the fruit! Trees have always been known by their fruit, but this time the tree was one that had no roots in the earth. In actual fact, it was one that had died then been raised to life again …life out from heaven, not from the earth. Now that's real priesthood!

Another time, towards the end, after the mourning for Aharon at Mount Hor, we began moving back towards the land, but we had to make a long detour around the land of Edom. That's the time we started complaining again. It's so often the way with any test of endurance, that those last miles, when the goal is almost in sight, are the hardest.

Well, Y'haveh heard our complaining and he sent us snakes. Poisonous snakes! Thousands of them! They were everywhere! People were getting bitten. We were dropping like leaves in the autumn.

We came to Moshe and confessed our sin and begged him to pray for us. And so he did. Y'haveh had him make a snake out of bronze, put it on a pole, and hold it up before the eyes of the people. When anyone was bitten, they would simply look at the snake on the pole …and they'd live.

To us, at that time, this was beyond understanding, but it was glorious! Y'haveh could save us from anything! Would he save us from the power of that ancient snake, the Devil? Would he even save us from ourselves? If so, then he truly could bring us into the land and cause us to possess it!

By the time we came to the Yarden at the end of the forty years, we had learnt the way of victory in the wilderness. On the way out, Y'haveh had gained glory over two kings through us! These were Sichon, king of the Emori who lived in Heshbon and 'Og, king of Bashan, who belonged to the remnant of the Refa'im.

At the borders of the land of promise, Moshe, the servant of Y'haveh died.

He ascended Mount N'vo, to the summit of Pisgah and there Y'haveh showed him all the land, but having failed the test, he was not allowed to enter.

At M'rivah Spring in the desert of Tzin, even after such an exodus, his faith had still needed a walking stick! Y'haveh had commanded him to speak to that rock; the one following; that it should produce its water, but instead he'd struck the rock with the rod.

Before he died, he pronounced a blessing on each of the tribes of Isra'el. He also laid his hands upon Y'hoshua ben Nun for the stewardship of the people, and Y'hoshua, my brother, was full of the spirit of wisdom.

By Colin Baker © 2007 All rights reserved

www.colininthespirit.com

The Gates of the Kingdom

~

A story of seed-time and harvest, of sprouting and blossoming, of bearing fruit with seed unto the fullness ... A Kingdom sown, a Kingdom reaped, a glorious Bride without spot or wrinkle, a matchless gift from a Father to a Son; bone of His bone and flesh of His flesh.

Heritage Series

The Jordan Gate

As the feet of the cohanim carrying the Ark entered the waters of the Yarden, the waters retreated from before the Lord. They banked up a great distance off at Adam. The waters flowing down to the sea of death were cut off. A dry crossing opened up in front of us, like a gateway to the land of promise.

The Lord holding back the waters, the people began to surge through the gate...

....

In the Heavenly Realm of Jesus Christ, there is a garden and a river.

The garden is full of peace and glory. The river flows with Life, and the Sh'khinah of the garden is reflected on the face of the waters.

The flow of the river swells and ebbs for its well-springs are in the living, breathing throne of the Lamb.

On a broad stretch of the waters of life, right on the edge of the water, a gate has appeared. It is a very great and mighty gate, and it is made of sapphire, deep and clear. Its foundations have just this moment been established upon the waters, and like the throne, it lives; it has the ability to 'expand' for it gives passage to the armies of Heaven…

....

When all the people and the Lord had come up out of the Yarden, we camped at Gilgal near Yericho. We named it Gilgal, (rolling,) because it was there that we circumcised all the boys and men who'd been born during our desert wanderings. It was there at Gilgal that Y'haveh said to the Ben Yisra'el; 'Today I have rolled the reproach of Egypt off of you.'…

....

In the Heavenly realm, there are stirrings at the sapphire gate. The River of Life has swollen all its banks. The armies of Heaven have assembled and

Jesus Christ, the Lord of Heaven's Armies, Adonai Tzva'ot in full battle dress, approaches the gate…

Giving physical expression to the Spirit of God as only He can do, He steps through. The armies follow and as they do, realms switch: The Heavenly Host look down on a muddy river in flood. In the distance, beyond the river; a walled city shut in. Their Lord is leading the way toward the city.

....

As they approach the wall, a command, and vast armies halt all around the city. Adonai Tzva'ot moves on alone. He ascends a small hill, drawing his sword as he goes. There, He stands waiting, resting the weight of His blade upon His shoulder.

Then, from the opposite slope, a challenge! Who would dare?!

"Are you for us, or for our enemies?!" There was a fire in the eyes of the challenger, and his hand was upon his sword.

Jesus turned and met Joshua eye to eye. "No! For I now come as the commander of the army of Y'haveh!"

Joshua fell on his face to the ground and worshiped. "What does Adonai have to say to his 'eved?"[13]

---

13 'eved: servant

"Take off your shoe, for the place on which you stand is holy; set aside for Y'haveh!"

As Joshua removed his shoes, the title deeds of Jericho passed into the right hand of Jehovah. Everything of Jericho was to be destroyed or become the possession of God. It was all holy.

Jericho was the first-fruits; the token for the whole grape harvest.

....

And all about the gate; armies from a realm unseen, the ruling realm, witnessed a transaction which Heaven would honor, and honor again.

....

The Jordan Gate II

Over five hundred years later, fifty mighty men, sons of the prophets of God, have gathered on that very same hill outside a re-built Jericho…

They are watching as their master Elijah, in company with his servant, Elisha, descends the slope towards the Jordan. They have assembled to bid their master farewell. It has become known both in the land of Israel and in Heaven above that his departure and arrival are imminent.

As they approach the river bank, Elisha senses the Spirit of Elohim, even of Adonai Tzva'ot coming with fire upon his master. He knew the sense well, for he had served him many years and a portion of his master's spirit was already his by association.

They embraced, but even as they did, Elisha knew that the spirit of his master was sensing the call to the other realm.

....

In Heavenly places, the host have assembled at the gate. There is a Spirit of Fire in every eye, and the gate begins to glow and to roll.

Like a great whirlwind, it funnels out above the waters of the river of Life.

....

Elijah releases Elisha, and with urgency he removes his cloak.

Rolling it up, he turns and swirling it over his head, he slams it down upon the face of the waters.

....

The mighty whirlwind plunges its tail through the waters, before the eyes of the host and of the One seated upon the Throne.

....

The waters part, the gate opens and the two step into the windswept doorway.

"Tell me;" says Elijah, shouting to make himself heard, "what shall I do for you before I am taken away?"

"Let two mouths of your spirit be mine, 'Avi; a double portion!"

"You ask a difficult thing, but if you see me when I'm being taken from you my ben, then your request shall be granted."

They ascend the far bank of the Jordan, and continue on…

....

The fiery gate begins folding in upon itself, and fire plunges down through the waters. The 'ben Elohim' ride through the gate!

....

As the two walk on together, trans-port arrives! They are separated by horses and chariots of fire, with the horsemen of the Kingdom riding in them. Elijah is taken up in a great "sap" (doorway, gate), like a mighty whirlwind (sa'ar), and Elisha is left gazing up into the heavens.

❊ ❊ ❊ ❊ ❊ ❊

In re-built Jericho, centuries later, the sons of the prophets come week by week to the synagogue, or is it a cathedral? For they come only at the chiming of a bell.

On this sunny spring morning, the people sit in cold pews. They have sung two songs, brought their offerings, sung another two songs, and sent the children out to Sabbath-school.

The priest rises, steps up to the podium, and looks around, eying his audience to make sure they're all awake and paying attention. He clears his throat and several droopy heads rise…

"The Scripture reading for today is Psalm ninety five ... that is: Psalm ... ninety ... five."

"O come, let us sing to Jehovah; let us make a joyful noise to the rock of our salvation. Let us come before His face with praise; let us shout for joy to Him with songs."

....

"For Jehovah is a great God and a great King above all gods."

"The deep places of the earth are in His hand; the summits of the mountains also are His."

"The sea is His and He made it; and His hands formed the dry land."

"O come, let us worship and bow down; let us kneel before Jehovah our maker. For he is our God and we are the people of His pasture, and the sheep of His hand."

"Today, if you will hear His voice, do not harden your heart as in Meribah; as in the day of Massah in the wilderness; when your fathers tempted Me, they tested Me and they saw My work. For forty years I was disgusted with this generation; and I said, 'They are a people who err in heart;' and, 'They do not know My ways,' to whom I swore in My anger, 'They shall not enter into My rest.'"

"Thump!" The priest closes the book and looks around.

Way down at the back of the audience, a brave young man has risen to his feet…

"Young brother Barnabas has a question. Please; speak."

....

"My brothers, if Y'hoshua had given us rest; why then does Adonai speak now of another day called 'today'? If He admonishes us not to harden our hearts today, then there remains another rest for the people of God to enter!"

"If we should by some means enter, what then shall be to the realms?"

....

"Guards!!! Guards!!! Arrest that man! He's dangerous! Arrest him at once! Lock him up and throw away the key!"

"What's going on?"

"I don't know."

"I don't know either."

"Somebody must have said something he didn't like!"

"Yeah, it was young Barnabas."

"What'd he say?"

"I don't know. I wasn't really listening."

....

You will no longer be spoken of as 'Azuvah (Abandoned) or your land be spoken of as 'Sh'mamah (Desolate); rather, you will be called Heftzi-Vah (My Delight Is In Her) and your land Be'ulah (Married). For Adonai delights in you and your land will be married. (Yesha'yahu 62:4 CJB)

❈ ❈ ❈ ❈ ❈

The River Gate

We sat down by the rivers of Babylon; also, we wept when we remembered Zion. (Psalms 137:1 LITV)

"…by the river Chebar, the heavens were opened and I saw visions of God." (Ezekiel 1:1b LITV)

"…as I was by the hand (beside or within the influence) of the great river, which is Tigris, then I lifted up my eyes and looked; and, behold…" (Daniel 10:4b-5a LITV)

And on the day of Sabbaths, we went outside the city beside a river, where it was customary for prayer to be made. (Acts 16:13 LITV)

✵ ✵ ✵ ✵ ✵

The 'Canal' Gate

"…in a vision I looked, and I was by the canal of Ulai," (Daniel 8:2b LITV)

✵ ✵ ✵ ✵ ✵

By Colin Baker © 2007 All rights reserved

www.colininthespirit.com

The Gates of the Kingdom

~

A story of seed-time and harvest, of sprouting and blossoming, of bearing fruit with seed unto the fullness ... A Kingdom sown, a Kingdom reaped, a glorious Bride without spot or wrinkle, a matchless gift from a Father to a Son; bone of His bone and flesh of His flesh.

Heritage Series

The Fire Gate

Part 1

In the beginning, God created the heavens and the earth ... and the earth had become a useless desolation, void of any life form. Darkness covered the face of the deep and the Ruwach; the Spirit; the Breath; the Life of Elohim, brooded over and against the face of those death waters, which, by their very state, were speaking against Him.

Then Elohim said, 'Let there be light' ...and there was light.

The darkness was pushed back into the depths of the waters by the light.

And Elohim saw the light, that it was good. And He made a distinction ...He separated between the light and the darkness.

And Elohim called the light, Day. And He called the darkness, Night. And there was evening, and there was morning; the first day.

And Elohim said, 'Let an expansive separation be made in the midst of the waters. Let it distinguish and divide between the waters oppressive and the waters oppressed; between the waters above and the waters below.' For the earth had become void and empty of inhabitable dwelling places (living things) *and spirits from both realms* (above and below) *had become, of necessity, contained and mixed within those anarchic waters.*

And Elohim made the expanse, as a boundary. He separated between the waters which were under the expanse and the waters which were above the expanse. And it was so.

And Elohim called the expanse, 'sky'. And there was evening, and there was morning; the second day...

....

Thousands of years and many generations later, the same Spirit is moving against the darkness of Babylon to separate light from darkness … To plant in human history, a seed … One that will bear fruit in its season, after its own kind…

"Ashpenaz[14]! …Summon Arioch to come before me."

"Yes, your Majesty."

The king's face is darkened by a frown. He is greatly disturbed within himself, and it has become known throughout the palace that serious trouble is brewing. Within minutes, the captain of the royal guard is bowing before the King…

"Arioch[15]: I have summoned you here into my presence that you might understand my decree. The Judean captive, Belt'shatzar[16], has asked for time. I have granted him a night. In the course of a night my decree shall not be diminished. Do you understand?"

"Yes, your Majesty."

"Confirm to me the command."

---

14 Ashpenaz: Chief Eunuch
15 Arioch: The captain of the king's guard
16 Belt'shatzar: Daniel; 'Protect His Life'

"If the 'ashshawph[17] do not reveal to my lord the king the dream and its meaning, they shall be cut to pieces, and their houses shall be made desolate so that they are used as latrines …your Majesty."

"Be sure to carry out my command fully. You are to make no distinction between the 'ashshawph. They and their entire households shall all be put to death, regardless of where they are from. If by the time of the morning sacrifice, they have not revealed the matter to me, they shall surely die."

"Yes, Your Majesty. It shall be done as you have commanded."

Out beyond the inner courtyard, against the outer wall of the palace stands a row of stone houses … And wafting out through windows and doorways, the sound of wailing; hysterical women; children crying …some silent. From the roof of the last dwelling, four young men ascend a ladder to the stairway of the battlements on the outer palace wall. Upon reaching a vacant catapult pad, they turn westward toward Jerusalem, kneel, and begin to pray, their faces to the ground. The sun has just dipped below the horizon and the sky is turning smoky red.

Well into the night they plead fervently for revelation; the revelation that will save their lives.

---

17 ashshawph: astrologers; wise men

Nothing happens. At the beginning of each new day, they have come here to pray, for they are captives; aliens in Babylon. This evening they have prayed far into the night with fervent pleadings and tears ... Silence.

One by one they sit up and one says, 'It is enough'. They rise and embrace one another. Their fate is no longer their concern. They have entrusted it to One greater than themselves. Their descent back to their house has in it the light hearted vigor of youth.

Only one lamp is extinguished in that row of stone houses and their sleep is swift and sweet ... Four young men on a large cushioned rug; Hananiah, Mishael, Azariah[18] and Daniel. They have been together from the beginning of their people's captivity.

As the Morning Star rises over the Palace, Daniel wakes with a shout… "Hallelujah!!!"

As the others rise, he falls on his face and blesses the God of heaven, for the Lord gave him a dream…

"Blessed be the name of Elohim

from eternity past to eternity future!

---

18   Hananiah, Mishael, Azariah: Shadrach, Meshach, Abednego

> For wisdom and power are his alone;
>
> he brings the changes of seasons and times;
>
> he installs and deposes kings;
>
> he gives wisdom to the wise
>
> and knowledge to those with discernment.
>
> He reveals deep and secret things;
>
> He knows what lies in the darkness;
>
> And light dwells with him.
>
> I thank and praise you, Elohim of my ancestors,
>
> for giving me wisdom and power,
>
> and revealing to me what we wanted from you,
>
> for giving us the answer for the king."

Now the dream and its interpretation await another day and another chapter for the telling ...

But, although the story of a rock and a people separated, tested and proven by the Spirit of God reaches far into the time of the end, it begins unfolding immediately. Our four young heroes, Hananiah, Mishael, Azariah and Daniel, rather than dying, were prospered greatly in a kingdom not their own ... All-be-it with much jealousy and antagonism from the locals …some of whom they saved that day, I might add.

So Daniel asked of the king, and he set Shadrach, Meshach and Abednego over the affairs of the province of Babylon … Honest young Jews over the affairs of an aging bureaucracy, steeped in long standing traditions of graft and corruption. But Daniel sat in the gate of the kingdom…

Now the king, Nebuchadnezzar, set up a great golden statue in the plain of Dura, beside the main road of the province of Babylon. He decreed that all peoples must bow down and worship it or face the fire. Perhaps you know the story. It was made of gold and was about thirty meters high …so it could be seen from a very great distance …

"It is complete. As you have commanded, so it has been done, your Majesty. No man, or god, will ever be able to break this statue to pieces."

"It bears my likeness Shazban. All people shall worship it for my glory and my pleasure. Anyone found not bowing down at the sound of any music shall be cast alive into the flaming furnace. The decree must be delivered to all peoples and provinces …then all things will be ready."

"Ashpenaz!"

"Your Majesty."

"You will now make arrangements for the dedication of the great golden image which I have set up. Call my scribe. I will make a decree. You shall have it copied and send also heralds into all the provinces."

Nebuwshazban, the king's 'ashpenaz' (chief eunuch), bows low and within minutes is back with the scribe.

"I, Nebuwkadnetstsar, King of Babel the Great, do this day command that all 'achashdarpan, all cegan, all pechah, all gedabar, all dethabar, all quwm, and all shiltown (the entire bureaucracy) shall present themselves for the dedication of the Great Golden Image, which I, their King have set up."

"Nebuwshazban will be responsible for the dispatch. You may go..."

Throughout the province of Babylon excitement is running high as the people look forward to the celebration and the feast. Thousands flock to the city from all the surrounding provinces ... Dancers, musicians, conjurers, acrobats, merchants and people of many languages. The city fills to overflowing as the day approaches and business has never been so good. The streets are crammed with stalls and displays. The noise of the merchants fills the air from daybreak till the mid-watch of the night.

In all this, Nebuwshazban is not the least bit perturbed. He simply entrusts matters into the hands of the most reliable prefects in Babylon. Yes… You guessed it; Shadrach, Meshach and Abednego…

"Misha'el, you worry too much. It will be alright. Has not Eloheinu himself placed us in authority? Don't worry. I will handle this problem."

"That's exactly what I was worried about brother. How do you plan to become invisible when a million people bow down and the three of us remain standing?"

"Latrines …I shall arrange latrines …many latrines, for the booths of the 'achashdarpan and the cegan."

"The cegan! The cegan don't have booths!"

"This time they shall …Less decorative than those of the princes, of course …But still; with latrines."

"'Ahi, I can feel the urge coming on already!"

"Yeah… Me too!" adds Azariah.

"Well then, it's settled. When the music is about to begin, we shall all get the urge."

"So be it brothers. Eloheinu has provided a way for us."

That very night, the king tosses and turns. He cannot sleep. Something is wrong. Something is not complete. There is some flaw, some weakness in the arrangements. The worship of his image must be established fully. Something is missing. The arrangements fall short of the objective …

"Nebuwshazban!!!"

Messengers scurry through lighted passageways. The king's ashpenaz emerges. Wiping his face with a scented towel, he tosses it to the messenger, and hurries into the chamber of the king.

"Your Majesty."

"It is not enough. The arrangements … They are insufficient."

"Your Majesty, I am at your service. Your every wish shall be carried out most thoroughly."

"Yes Shazban, I know that I can rely on you. You have served me well for many years. I want you to arrange for musicians. Musicians shall sound music throughout Babylon. There shall be music in all the streets and marketplaces of the city for the entire course of this moon. And in the palace Shazban … There shall be music heard in the palace three times every day. I want all the people to bow down to my image. Any dissent shall be totally purged from my kingdom. The fire shall be the only place for dissenters. Do you understand?"

"Yes, Your Majesty. It shall be as you have commanded."

"Oh! One other thing… Make it known that those who report dissenters shall be rewarded."

"Your Majesty."

"Goodnight Shazban."

"Yes, goodnight … Sleep well your Majesty."

I will not bore you with pomp and ceremony and long, long speeches. Needless to say, Hananiah's ploy worked well. The king himself did not notice their refusal to bow down to a strange god …Nor did any of the other officials; on that day.

Daniel had been kept very much in their prayers, and they in his throughout this season of testing. But for the four of them, there was also another name that took precedence over their own…

"…for your name's sake O Elohim, do not allow the wicked to prosper over those who bear your name. Do not allow any foreign god to exult itself over your name. Honor and glory and majesty belong to you. We will worship no other god; because of your name. Your name, Elohim, is most holy to us and we will not defile your holy name."

"You know Adonai that we stood this day. You know that we were seen to stand when all the king's officials bowed down. Spare us O Elohim, the test. You know our hearts are pure before you, even so, do with us as you wish. May our lives be in your hands and yours alone, O Eloheinu."

The next day, the Chaldean treasurers and other officials went together, and approached the king…

"May the king live forever! Your Majesty, you have ordered that everyone who hears the sound of the horn, pipe, harp, zither, lute, bagpipe and the rest of the musical instruments must fall down and worship the gold statue; and that whoever does not fall down and worship will be thrown into a blazing hot furnace. There are some Jews, whom you have put in charge of the affairs of the province of Bavel; Shadrakh, Meishakh, and 'Aved-N'go … and these men, your majesty, have paid no attention to you. They do not serve your gods and they do not worship the gold statue you set up."

Nebuchadnezzar, in raging fury, commanded that the three be brought before him immediately …

"Shadrakh! Meishakh! 'Aved-N'go! Is it true that you neither serve my gods nor worship the gold statue I set up? All right, then … If you are prepared, when you hear the sound of the musical instruments, to fall down and worship the gold statue; very well …But if you won't worship, you will immediately be thrown into a blazing hot furnace – and what god will save you from my power then?"

"Your majesty, your question doesn't require an answer from us. If our God whom we serve can save us, he will save us from the blazing hot furnace and from your power. But even if he doesn't, we want you to know, your majesty, that we will neither serve your gods nor worship the gold statue which you have set up."

The face of the king turned dark crimson with rage as the spirits directing him began reacting against the presence of one so different to themselves …a spirit more impregnable than any fortress. He ground his teeth and his face distorted …

"By the gods of Bavel, the furnace shall be seven times hotter than ever before or you will all be thrown into it!!!"

"Arioch!!! Arioch!!! I want my champions!!! I want them now!!! Now!!! Do you hear me? Arioch!!!"

"Yes, your Majesty! Immediately, your Majesty!"

"Bind them!!! And get them out of my sight."

"I will see the three of you writhing in the flames this very hour!!!"

Arioch re-appears with three warriors of very great stature…

❊ ❊ ❊ ❊ ❊

The Gates of the Kingdom

~

A story of seed-time and harvest, of sprouting and blossoming, of bearing fruit with seed unto the fullness ... A Kingdom sown, a Kingdom reaped, a glorious Bride without spot or wrinkle, a matchless gift from a Father to a Son; bone of His bone and flesh of His flesh.

Heritage Series

The Fire Gate

Part 2

"Your Majesty ... your champions:"

"Ah... Yes! Come forward. You three are the strongest warriors in the world. You shall represent my power over my enemies and over the gods of my enemies. This very morning I wish to display my power, and you shall be my executioners. You shall tie my three enemies, Shadrakh, Meishakh and Aved-N'go, securely, so that they cannot move their arms or legs.

You shall carry them up the hurling ramp of the furnace before my face and you shall hurl them all the way to the very centre of the flames."

An evil smile creeps across their faces and the three bow before their king. They depart to the detention chamber, where our three young heroes are waiting and praying under armed guard…

"Just like the burnt offerings of rams and bullocks, and just as in multitudes of fat lambs, so let our sacrifice be in your sight this day. Grant that we may wholly follow you …for they shall not be confounded that put their trust in you. We follow you with all our heart. We fear you, and seek your face."

Ropes are brought, and the three of them are bound securely from head to foot. The scene is rather strange, since the three boys are so radically dwarfed by their executioners …and so submissive …Like little lambs.

Hananiah, Mishael and Azariah just look at one another. They speak not a word. Each knows that he shall meet his God in but a few moments of time.

All the princes and the king's officials have been summoned to the court of Zamama[1] by urgent decree, to witness the execution by fire. The witness

---

1   Zamama: A Babylonian deity associated with Ishtar; worshiped in the courtyard of Marduk

stand is full. The king enters with his entourage and all the people stand and bow, taking care not to sit until the king himself sits down.

The priests, dressed in their best ceremonial robes, parade around the furnace, where wood has been piled up around the inner periphery so high that it has reached even the level of the platform of hurling itself. Ten, dressed in red garments, descend into the furnace bearing torches. They come out, running!

Smoke begins to ascend. The flames leap up, fueled on by the sacrificial rosin, by pitch and by masses of kindling wood. The doorway of the ramp swings open and the priests line up either side of the ramp-way.

The king's champions appear; each carrying their victim fully dressed and bound head to foot. The king holds up his hand. His face has not changed. The flames are not yet hot enough. They wait.

From the foot of the ramp, Hananiah, Mishael and Azariah can see the flames beginning to appear out from the opening, leaping up above the platform of hurling. They feel the heat on their faces …So also do those in the witness stand. The whole pantheon begins heating up. The three great warriors look to their king. His face is not changed. Nebuchadnezzar holds up his hand. They wait.

The flames leap up way above the platform and everyone is beginning to get scorched by the heat. The king gives the command with his rod. The three warriors begin their ascent of the ramp towards the platform of hurling.

The heat is so intense that the mighty men of the king actually use their three victims as shields to protect themselves as they approach the platform at the opening of the furnace.

But with Hananiah, Mishael and Azariah, something strange is happening. They feel no heat …Yet the ropes that bind them are beginning to smoke. They look across at one another… One last look… They have not yet realized what is really going on.

They reach the platform, and the ropes are bursting into flame. Three very big warriors are finding their 'shields' a bit small for them. They run at the place of hurling, the heat scorching their legs and shoulders.

Hurling the three boys with all their might, they are suddenly hit by heat indescribable. They burst into flame and collapse on the platform; dead … and alight. A cry of shocked horror goes up from the witnesses. The smell of burning flesh is added to the smoke of the furnace.

The three land together on the inner platform of the furnace. All around them the fire is raging …the light of it blinding to their eyes for a while. The ropes binding them are burning fiercely. Still they feel no heat! Then something happens that will forever set their destinies in place … Someone helps them each to their feet, speaking words of comfort to them…

....

"Misha'el, Azaryah, Hananyah … Don't be afraid, for I have redeemed you. I am calling you by name for you are mine. When you pass through water, I will be with you. When you pass through rivers, they will not overwhelm you. When you walk through fire, you will not be scorched. The flame will not burn you. I am with you."

As their eyes adjust, they can see him. Not an angel, but a man … a young man …Like them, but regal … Glorious beyond description. But his words… they are not new to them. They know the source of these words …And now, they see Him! …Yet they live! In the fire, by the presence of their God, they live!!!

They look at each other… They are covered in the glowing embers of the rope. They brush them off. Sparks and dust falling all around. Their clothes are not harmed!!! They give their garments a good shaking ...more dust. They are clean. The fire has not touched them!!! In the realization of reality, they fall down and at the feet of their Lord, worshipping with one voice...

> *"Blessed are you, O Adonai, God of our fathers: and to be praised and exalted above all for ever. And blessed is your glorious and holy name ... To be praised and exalted above all for ever.*
>
> *Blessed are you in the temple of your holy glory ... To be praised and glorified above all for ever.*
>
> *Blessed are you who sees the depths, and sits upon the cherubim ... To be praised and exalted above all for ever.*
>
> *Blessed are you on the glorious throne of your kingdom ... To be praised and glorified above all for ever.*
>
> *Blessed are you in the firmament of heaven ... Above all to be praised and glorified for ever.*

O all you works of the Lord, bless the Lord ... Praise and exalt him above all for ever.

O you heavens, bless the Lord ... Praise and exalt him above all for ever.

O you angels of the Lord, bless the Lord ... Praise and exalt him above all for ever.

O all you waters that be above the heaven, bless the Lord ... Praise and exalt him above all for ever.

O all you powers of the Lord, bless the Lord ... Praise and exalt him above all for ever.

O you sun and moon, bless the Lord ... Praise and exalt him above all for ever.

O you stars of heaven, bless the Lord ... Praise and exalt him above all for ever.

O every shower and dew, bless the Lord ... Praise and exalt him above all for ever.

O all you winds, bless the Lord ... Praise and exalt him above all for ever.

O you fire and heat, bless the Lord ... Praise and exalt him above all for ever.

O you winter and summer, bless the Lord ... Praise and exalt him above all for ever.

O you dews and storms of snow, bless the Lord ... Praise and exalt him above all for ever.

O you nights and days, bless the Lord ... Praise and exalt him above all for ever.

O you light and darkness, bless the Lord ... Praise and exalt him above all for ever.

O you ice and cold, bless the Lord ... Praise and exalt him above all for ever.

O you frost and snow, bless the Lord ... Praise and exalt him above all for ever.

O you lightnings and clouds, bless the Lord ... Praise and exalt him above all for ever.

O let the earth bless the Lord ... Praise and exalt him above all for ever.

O you mountains and little hills, bless the Lord ... Praise and exalt him above all for ever.

O all things that grow in the earth, bless the Lord ... Praise and exalt him above all for ever.

O you mountains, bless the Lord ... Praise and exalt him above all for ever.

O you seas and rivers, bless the Lord ... Praise and exalt him above all for ever.

O you whales, and all that move in the waters, bless the Lord ... Praise and exalt him above all for ever.

O you fowl of the air, bless the Lord ... Praise and exalt him above all for ever.

O you beasts and cattle, bless the Lord ... Praise and exalt him above all for ever.

O you children of men, bless the Lord ... Praise and exalt him above all for ever.

O Israel, bless the Lord ... Praise and exalt him above all for ever.

O you priests of the Lord, bless the Lord ... Praise and exalt him above all for ever.

O you servants of the Lord, bless the Lord ... Praise and exalt him above all for ever.

O you spirits and souls of the righteous, bless the Lord ... Praise and exalt him above all for ever.

O you holy and humble men of heart, bless the Lord ... Praise and exalt him above all for ever.

O Hananyah, 'Azaryah, and Misha'el, bless the Lord ... Praise and exalt him above all for ever ... For he has delivered us from hell, and saved us from the hand of death, and delivered us in the midst of the furnace and burning flame: even in the midst of the fire has he delivered us!

O give thanks to the Lord, because he is gracious ... For his mercy endures for ever!

O all you that worship the Lord, bless the God of gods, praise him, and give him thanks ... For his mercy endures for ever!

The three of them, filled with unbridled joy, continue to exult in their Lord and in their being with him in the flames.

....

As they begin to move about, they start to become sometimes visible to the officials witnessing their 'execution'. People begin to point.

Nebuchadnezzar jumps to his feet, staring into the flames. Incredulous at the sight, he exclaims, "Look!!! Didn't we throw three men bound into the flames!!!?"

"Yes. Of course, Your Majesty!"

"But look!!! Look there!!! I see four men walking about freely in the flames ... unharmed!!! And the fourth is like a son of the gods!!!"

Completely forgetting all protocol, Nebuchadnezzar runs to the ramp, and cautiously approaches the mouth of the furnace, shielding his face from the heat with his hands. He edges as close as he dares and calls out...

"Shadrakh! Meishakh! 'Aved-N'go! You servants of the Most High God! Come out and come here!"

Hananiah, Mishael and Azariah ascend from the flames. Stepping over the smoking remains of the king's champions, they present themselves before Nebuchadnezzar, the king. Their faces are aglow with the joy of their Lord. All the king's officials gather around them and are amazed to see that their hair, their clothes and their bodies have not been affected by the fire. There is not even the smell of fire on them.

Realizing the truth, Nebuchadnezzar glorifies God as all his demons flee from before the light of reality made plain to see…

"Blessed be the God of Shadrakh, Meishakh and Aved-N'go! He has sent his angel and delivered his servants. They trusted in him, and defied the royal command even to the point of being willing to give up their bodies that they might not serve or worship any god other than their own! Therefore I decree that any person from any nation or language who says anything amiss about the god of Shadrakh, Meishakh and 'Aved-N'go shall be cut to pieces, and his house shall be made into a latrine …For there is no other god who is able to save like this!!!"

Then the king made Hananiah, Mishael and Azariah prosper in the province of Babylon.

....

…For just as the Messiah's sufferings overflow into us, so through the Messiah our encouragement also overflows. So if we undergo trials, it is for

your encouragement and deliverance; and if we are encouraged, that should encourage you when you have to endure sufferings like those we are experiencing. Moreover, our hope for you remains staunch, because we know that as you share in the sufferings, you will also share in the encouragement. (2 Corinthians 1:5-10 JNT)

...For as often as you eat this bread and drink the cup, you proclaim the Lord's death until he comes. (1 Corinthians 11:26 NASU)

...But each one's work will be shown for what it is; the Day will disclose it, because it will be revealed by fire – the fire will test the quality of each one's work. If the work someone has built on the foundation (Messiah) survives, he will receive a reward; if it is burned up, he will have to bear the loss: he will escape with his life, but it will be like escaping through a fire. (Ref. 1 Corinthians 3:13-15 JNT)

...But those who can discern will shine like the brightness of the heaven's dome, and those who turn many to righteousness like the stars forever and ever. (Daniel 12:3 CJB)

"They will be mine," says ADONAI-Tzva'ot, "on the day when I compose my own special treasure. I will spare them as a man spares his own son who serves him. Then once again you will see the difference between the righteous and the wicked, between the

person who serves God and one that doesn't serve him. For the day is coming, burning like a furnace, when all the proud and evildoers will be stubble; the day that is coming will set them ablaze," says ADONAI-Tzva'ot, "and leave them neither root nor branch. But to you who fear my name, the sun of righteousness will rise with healing in its wings; and you will break out leaping, like calves released from the stall. You will trample the wicked, they will be ashes under the soles of your feet on the day when I take action," says ADONAI-Tzva'ot. (Malachi 3:17-4:3 CJB)

By Colin Baker © 2007 All rights reserved

www.colininthespirit.com

The Gates of the Kingdom

~

A story of seed-time and harvest, of sprouting and blossoming, of bearing fruit with seed unto the fullness ... A Kingdom sown, a Kingdom reaped, a glorious Bride without spot or wrinkle, a matchless gift from a Father to a Son; bone of His bone and flesh of His flesh.

Heritage Series

The Gate in Session

"Israelites; whose are the adoption" (Romans 9:4a LITV) "And I said, 'Let them set a clean turban on his head.'" (Zechariah 3:5a LITV)

Shalom a lei-khem, my name is Z'kharyah. I am the son of Berekhyah, and the grandson of 'Iddo, the prophet.

Since so few have made mention of our custom, it has fallen to me to enlighten those of you who look for the ancient paths and who search for the ways of Tzion.

To begin my dod, I shall speak to you of my experience in the realm below. I shall speak of those days when the ceremony of adoption was still practiced in the gates of Yisra'el, as in the gates of the Kingdom.

For every man with sons, there will come a day for the passing on of name, authority, position and of course, his place in the gate. Well, towards that day, a wise father will discipline and train his sons, particularly the first-born.

Now, I've known sons to reject their father's discipline. If the father had any sense at all; they missed out. If a rebellious son is to receive adoption, then the father actually must lie in the gate. Before the elders of the town and before the prophet or priest of Adonai, he would have to lie in order for that to happen.

I have known of some to be so desperate and foolish. They all suffered ... great loss.

This then is how it works; the adoption of sons: When a father is fully satisfied in his son; a son who has willingly received all his father's instruction and discipline ... when that time has fully come, he will clothe his son with rich ceremonial garments and bring him to the city gate.

The young man will bring his friends. There, in the presence of witnesses, the town elders, priests or Adonai's prophet, the father will say to the witnesses; 'This is my son in whom I am well pleased; listen to him[2].'

At this point, I would usually say, 'Crown him... Put a new turban on his head.'

Then, turning to his son, the father will himself set the turban on his head. This will be of matching design and color to the father's own and to his father's before him. It speaks of the father's way of thinking. Then he will say to the son; 'You are my son, today I have begotten you,' or, 'today I have become your father[3].'

These two statements which the father makes are of very great significance. The first says that the father has passed on all of his authority to the son. The second says that up until this day, people have approached the son through the father. From this day on, people must approach the father through the son. The son now speaks for the father, and the father's will is now to be known through the son.

The fact that it is done in the gate makes the transaction legal and binding.

This, my 'ah, my 'ahot, is the meaning of adoption to the ben Yisra'el.

---

2   See Matthew 3:17 and 17:5
3   See Psalms 2:7

This much forgotten custom of our people is however just a shadow; a picture of something very, very real and much more glorious.

Back in the time of my own spiritual discipline, in the second year of the reign of Daryavesh, during the month of Sh'vat, Adonai Tzva'ot came to me in visions of the night…

He made me to see Joshua the high priest standing before the Angel of Jehovah, (The one who speaks for Y'haveh) *and Satan standing at his right hand to accuse him.*

And Jehovah said to Satan, Jehovah rebuke you, Satan! And, Jehovah who has chosen Jerusalem rebuke you!

Is not this a brand plucked out of the fire?

And Joshua was clothed with filthy garments. They were all covered in dung and they stunk badly. I came to know those priestly garments well. They were spattered with my blood one day between the porch and the altar. His pride in those vestments and their testimony made him repulsive in the presence of the 'Angel'. And he stood before the Angel.

And He answered and spoke to those who stood before Him, (the witnesses) *saying, Take away the filthy garments from him.*

And He said to him, Behold, I have caused your iniquity to pass from you, and I will clothe you with ceremonial robes.

And I said; Let them set a clean turban on his head. And they set a clean turban on his head and clothed him with clothing. And the Angel of Jehovah stood by.

And the Angel of Jehovah charged Joshua, saying, So says Jehovah of Hosts, (Adonai Tzva'ot) *If you will walk in My ways, and if you will keep My charge, then you shall also judge My house, and shall also keep My courts; and I will give you room to walk among these who stand by.*

These were all immaculately dressed in the richest of garments, with golden turbans upon their heads; they were the ben Elohim! Adonai Tzva'ot was offering him Son-ship!!!

Hear now, O Joshua the high priest, you and your friends who are sitting before you, for they are men of symbol, For, behold, I will bring forth My servant, the Branch ...

In one way, these were symbols of things to come, but for me they have already come. I am one who has been through the gate. I can assure you my 'ah, my 'ahot, because Yeshua, the Branch has now already come, that same offer is also extended to you!

Don't assume that Son-ship is just a new relationship that comes with your heavenly birth. It goes much further than that. Relationship comes by birth, but Son-ship by 'adoption'.

Son-ship is worth any price!

'Y'varekh'kha Adonai v' yishmerekha.

(May Adonai bless you and keep you.)

Ya'er Adonai panav eleikha vichunekka.

(May Adonai make His face shine on you and show you His favor)

Yissa Adonai panav eleikha v'yasem l'kha shalom.

(May Adonai lift up His face toward you and give you peace.)

✻ ✻ ✻ ✻ ✻

* Author's footnote: "Some of my best sons are daughters."

By Colin Baker © 2007 All rights reserved

www.colininthespirit.com

The Gates of the Kingdom

~

A story of seed-time and harvest, of sprouting and blossoming, of bearing fruit with seed unto the fullness ... A Kingdom sown, a Kingdom reaped, a glorious Bride without spot or wrinkle, a matchless gift from a Father to a Son; bone of His bone and flesh of His flesh.

Heritage Series

The Little Gate of the Great King

Part 1

...And God said, Let the earth sprout tender sprouts, the plant seeding seed, the fruit tree producing fruit according to its kind, whichever seed is in it on the earth. And it was so. And the earth bore tender sprouts, the plant seeding seed according to its kind, and the fruit tree producing fruit according to its kind, whichever seed is in it. And God saw that it was good...

And God said, Let the waters swarm with swarmers having a soul of life; and let the birds fly over the earth, on the face of the expanse of the heavens. And God created the great sea animals, and all that creeps, having a living soul, which swarmed the waters, according to its kind; and every bird with wing according to its kind. And God saw that it was good. And God blessed them, saying, Be fruitful and multiply, and fill the waters in the seas; and let the birds multiply in the earth...

And God said, Let the earth bring forth the soul of life according to its kind: cattle, and creepers, and its beasts of the earth, according to its kind. And it was so. And God made the beasts of the earth according to its kind, and cattle according to its kind, and all creepers of the ground according to its kind. And God saw that it was good.

And God said, let Us make man in Our image, according to Our likeness; and let them rule over the fish of the sea, and over the birds of the heavens, and over the cattle, and over all the earth, and over all the creepers creeping on the earth. And God created the man in His own image; in the image of God He created him. He created them male and female. And God blessed them; and God said to them, Be fruitful and multiply, and fill the earth, and subdue it, and rule over the fish of the seas, and over birds of the heavens, and over all beasts creeping on the earth...

And God saw everything that He had made and behold, it was very good. (Genesis 1:11-31 extracts LITV)

"For the earth will be filled with the knowledge of the glory of the Lord, as the waters cover the sea." (Habakkuk 2:14 NASU)

Every seed that sprouts, every flower bud that opens, every bird that sings, gives testimony to the fact that God's desire is fulfilled in it ...to his glory! And in that glory they exult with their Creator ...full of life. Together their spirits are ascendant as they dance the dance of the double helix; the dance of life[4] ...

"Ahh ...the lot falls to Z'kharyah! So be it 'ah. Adonai has chosen. Z'kharyah shall offer up the 'Shemoneh Esrei' with incense before Adonai."

A rumble of agreement rolls around the circle, and the Priests of Abijah disburse, leaving one aged priest staring at the lot with a questioning look in his eyes.

---

4   dance of life: When spirits dance together, there is a pattern; the pattern of life. CRB

It had been a very long time since he had been chosen …A time of deep perplexity and of crying out to God, the Father of all.

Zechariah's deep longing; his ceaseless prayer to father a son was somewhat raw after keeping the recent fast. Hope itself had long since died in him, but each time God moved in his life, something stirred deep inside and brought a tear to his weary eyes. Still; he dared not hope.

When the time came, he found that there were more people praying in the courtyard than usual and even the court of the women was full. This did not surprise the aged priest one little bit. He knew that the people had come to cry out to God for relief from their oppressors …and from the lawlessness that pervaded Judea.

They trusted that on this day he would smell the fragrant incense offered, and hear their cry …and maybe even answer their prayer. It was all they could do. There was no other hope. All other hopes had been dashed by the sword until hope itself had almost died. But deep inside, something still embraced a hope in God …Age old promises of a deliverer who would come from God himself to redeem his people; Israel, and set them free … The Messiah!

He approached the doorway to the inner court…

Having entered into the sanctuary alone, he takes the burning incense and places it upon that small golden altar which stood before the curtain …and begins to pray the 'Shemoneh Esrei', as was the custom …

> "Blessed are you, Adonai Eloheinu, God of 'avoteinu (our fathers), Elohei Avraham, Elohei Yitzchak vElohei Ya'akov, the great, mighty and revered El 'Elyon, who gives kindnesses plentiful, the creator of all, who recalls the good deeds of the 'avot and who brings a Redeemer to their children's children for his name's sake, in love. O king, helper, savior and shield. Blessed are you Adonai, the shield of Avraham."

> "You, Adonai, are mighty forever. You are the reviver of the dead. You are greatly able to save. You cause the wind to blow and the rain to fall. You sustain the living in loving-kindness. You revive the dead with great compassion. You support the falling, heal the sick, set free the bound and keep faith with those who sleep in the dust. Who is like you O master of mighty deeds? Who compares to you, a king who puts

to death and restores to life, and brings forth salvation?"

"...Return us 'Avinu, to your Torah; draw us near, our King, to serve you. Restore us to your presence in complete repentance. Blessed are you Adonai ... you desire repentance."

"Forgive us 'Avinu, for we have sinned; pardon us, our King, for we have rebelled ... Blessed are you Adonai, the gracious one, who abundantly forgives."

"Behold our affliction and champion our cause, and redeem us speedily for the sake of thy Name. Blessed are you, Adonai, Redeemer of Yisra'el."

"Heal us Adonai, and we shall be healed; save us and we will be saved, for you are the one we praise. Bring complete healing for all our sicknesses. May it be your will, Adonai Elohei, Elohei 'Avoteinu, that you send complete healing from Heaven to Elisheva, along with all others who suffer in Yisra'el, for you are our faithful and compassionate Healer and King. Blessed are you, Adonai, Our Healer."

"Sound the great shofar for our freedom, and raise a banner to gather our exiles … Blessed are you Adonai, who re-gathers the scattered of his people, Yisra'el."

"…And may you establish the throne of David in Yerushalayim without delay. Blessed are you Adonai, the Builder of Yerushalayim."

"May the seed of thy servant David flourish without delay and may you exult in your salvation. For in your salvation we hope all the day. Blessed are you Adonai, who brings forth the Horn of our salvation."

"…Blessed are you Adonai, who restores his presence to Tziyon."

"…You are the Rock and Shield of our salvation, you alone from generation to generation … Every day your miracles are with us; your wonders and favors always, evening, morning, and afternoon. We put our hope in you. For all these things we bless and exult your Name, our King, without ceasing. And all the living shall confess you forever and praise your Name in truth, O God of our salvation and our help forever! Blessed are you Adonai, 'The Good One' is your Name. To you it is right to give thanks."

"Grant peace, blessing, goodness, grace, kindness and compassion upon us and upon all your people Yisra'el. Bless us 'Avinu, all of us as one, with the light of your face, for with the light of your face you gave to us, Adonai Eloheinu, the Torah of life and love …of kindness, righteousness, blessing, compassion, life and peace. Blessed are you Adonai, who blesses his people Yisra'el with shalom."

As is the custom of the Priests, Zechariah turns to his left, bows, and prays: "He who makes peace in his heights…" then turning back, he bows forward towards the incense altar, the curtain and the presence beyond, and prays: "May he make shalom upon us…" then straightening his aged back: "and upon all Yisra'el …Amen."

As he opens his eyes …light! There! Right in front of him! To the right of the altar! Stands a mighty angel of God! Startled and terrified at the sight, the old man almost falls over backwards.

"Don't be afraid Z'kharyah. Your prayer has been heard[5]. Your wife, Elisheva, will bear you a son. You shall name him Yochanan. He will be a great joy to you and your delight will be in him. Many people will rejoice when he is born because he will be great in the sight of Adonai."

"He is never to drink wine or any other liquor."

"He will be filled with the Ruach HaKodesh, even from his mother's womb."

"He will turn many of the people of Isra'el to their God."

"He will go ahead of Adonai in the spirit and power of Eliyahu, to turn the hearts of the 'avot[6] to their ben[7], and the disobedient to the wisdom of the righteous; to prepare a people for Adonai."

"By w what can I b be sh shore of th th this. I I am an old m m man. My w wife; sh she is w well on in y years?"

"I am Gavri'el! I stand in the presence of Y'haveh! I was sent! …to speak to you; to give you this good

---

5   See Luke 1:13 JNT. If the offering of the Shemoneh Esrei fell on a regular Sabbath, (as it did in the year 4BC), the priest offering it was allowed the special privilege of mentioning a family member by name in his prayer.
6   'avot: fathers
7   ben: sons; children

news. What I have said will be fulfilled in its season, but because you didn't believe my words, you will be silent. You will be completely incapable of speech until these things take place."

※ ※ ※ ※ ※

Six months later, at the time of the Feast of the Dedication, in Nazareth – Galilee of the Gentiles – Mary retires to her room for the night.

She cherishes the joy they have just shared together around the meal table …Her father's telling of all the favorite stories of the Maccabees liberation and the dedication of God's Temple.

She cherishes the warmth of hope that was kindled in them as her mother lit the memorial candles. It was a tradition with her people that a woman should bring the light into the home on such occasions.

For Mary, there is one more light of hope to be lit each night before she goes to bed. After tucking in her little sister, she takes a small oil lamp from its place on the window sill, bounces down the stairs, and pours in a little oil to the broad grins and knowing smiles of her kin who are still sitting around the table telling stories and sharing in the wine. With hardly a hint of embarrassment, she goes to the table, lights the lamp off the festive candle, and skips back up the stairs, knowing full well the laughter and comment she has aroused in the guests.

She places the small lamp in the window, as she has done every night since her betrothal to Yosef at Tabernacles two long months before. It is a sign to her bridegroom that she is ready …but tonight, more than that, it is a sign of an undying hope in her people; a hope of salvation, and a hope where joy resides when all around is darkness and gloom.

In stark contrast to the warm glow of their home, the night beyond her window was dark … even the moon was dimmed by cloud. She knew it would rain before morning and she was not fond of rainy nights.

Mary lay down, but not really for sleep. The loft was warm and it felt good to put her feet up. She could hear the rowdy voices of Uncle Ammon and her father downstairs as the wine loosened their tongues just a little more than usual. They were both very reserved men on any normal day.

She knew that Yosef would not come for her that night. Apart from the rain, she had seen him that very afternoon, and it was a custom for the groom not to see his bride for at least a week before the marriage. In some ways she had been disappointed to see him, but glad at the same time. Still, she chose to place the candle in the window. It was special to her, and it had become a witness also between her and Adonai. Each night she placed it with a prayer for Yosef and herself, and for her people.

It was long after the last voices had departed the gate, the air had chilled, and the front door latch finally dropped that she felt ready for sleep.

Suddenly, she sensed a strange light in the room, as if the moon was shining brightly through the window. Startled, she turned and sat up. There, beside her lamp, stood an angel …shining with the glory of God!

Gabriel approached closer. Mary braced herself and swung her feet to the floor, but was too afraid to rise before such an awesome being of light…

"Shalom, recipient of surrounding grace! Adonai is with you! You are blessed among women!"

"Don't be afraid Miryam, for you have found favor with Ha'Elyon. Behold; you will conceive in your womb and bear a son! You shall name him Yeshua. He will be great, and will be called Ben-Ha'Elyon. Adonai Elohim will give him the throne of his father, David, and he will rule over the house of Ya'akov to the ages. His Kingdom shall never end!"

"How shall this happen?! I am a virgin!"

"The Ruach HaKodesh will come upon you, and the power of Ha'Elyon will overshadow you ...So the holy child born to you will be called Ben-Elohim."

"Your doda[8], Elisheva, who is advanced in years - everyone says she is barren - she has conceived a son, and is six months pregnant. With Y'haveh, nothing is impossible!"

Bowing at the Name, Mary responds out of heartfelt adoration and fear of her God...

"Behold, I am the bond-servant of Adonai. May it be done to me as you have said."

With those simple words, on this night, Mary has 'dedicated her temple'.

Gabriel turns, and in the blink of an eye, he is gone.

Mary will never be the same again. She has committed herself to the 'non-impossible'!

She is not sure how she managed to say such words, and incredulously ponders the sound of her own voice saying what she said!

One thing she knows for sure; she must see Elisheva straight away.

* * * * *

8 doda: beloved relative

The Gates of the Kingdom

~

A story of seed-time and harvest, of sprouting and blossoming, of bearing fruit with seed unto the fullness ... A Kingdom sown, a Kingdom reaped, a glorious Bride without spot or wrinkle, a matchless gift from a Father to a Son; bone of His bone and flesh of His flesh.

Heritage Series

The Little Gate of the Great King

Part 2

As they prepare breakfast, Mary and her mother, find themselves alone. The men are a little late in rising. She decides to take the chance...

"'Em[9]?"

"Yes, Precious ... What troubles you?"

---

9   Em: Mother

"Oh, nothing really, I was just wondering about Doda Elisheva. We haven't seen her in a long time. Have you heard any news of her lately?"

Mary's mother covers the jar of goat's milk she was about to pour and looks very thoughtfully at Mary…

"Elisheva and Z'kharyah are at home at their house in the hill country. Your dod has lost his voice and I've heard that Elisheva is not well either."

"Not well? Is that all? She might be very sick! What if she's dying? She could be dying and we wouldn't even know about it!"

"Oh Miryam, don't be silly. If she were dying, someone would have told us. None of the guests said anything about the matter last night. Why are you so concerned about your doda, Elisheva, all of a sudden?"

"'Imi (my mother)!? We should all be concerned if she's not well."

"Yosef is going that way tomorrow. He has some work to do out there. I thought it might be nice if I paid her a visit. That way I could bring back news of how she really is."

"Ahh-ha! So, that's what you're up to! I knew there'd be something like that going on."

"Miryam; it's raining, and the roads are a mess. What makes you think your 'av is going to let you go out in such conditions?"

"'Em, I just thought we could talk about it. It's a matter of trust really."

"You know full well that we trust you …and Joseph. That's not the point! What about other people who see you gallivanting about the countryside together? It's just not on!"

Just then, Mary's father comes in, lays aside his walking stick, and sits down at the table…

"What's not on? Is there something going on here that I should know about?"

"Oh, 'Avi; it's Elisheva… She's not well and I just want to go and visit her. Please, 'Avi!!!"

"It's raining."

"Not now 'Avi; tomorrow … Yosef is going that way. I could go with him, and 'ahoti[10] could be chaperon."

"And what makes you think it won't be raining tomorrow young lady?"

"So, I can go then, if the sun is shining?!"

---

10 'ahoti: my sister

"Miryam, it has rained every morning for the last week. But if you insist, then you can go if the sun shines in the morning …only if the sun shines … and no arguments. I don't want to hear anything more about the matter."

"Oh, thank you 'Avi!" exclaims Mary, leaping up to kiss her father, planting a smile on his face that meets with quite a different kind of look from his wife…

"It will rain. Don't worry woman!"

That night by the lamp, Mary makes two requests of her Lord: forgiveness for misleading her parents, and sunshine in the morning. Both requests are granted. She is the recipient of surrounding grace.

The next day the two Marys walk out into brilliant morning light to break the news to Joseph about their journey into the hill country to visit Elizabeth, leaving their mum and dad to sort out their little differences at home.

Late afternoon finds them in the courtyard of Zechariah, who had been sitting with his nephew, the son of Hezir, making a shopping list of sorts on a slate. Joseph sits down with the men while Mary goes in to Elizabeth and her sister goes with Salome, their cousin's wife, to the kitchen.

When Elizabeth heard Mary's greeting, the baby in her womb leapt and she was filled with the Holy Spirit. She cried out: "Of all women, you are being blessed. How blessed is the child in your womb!"

"But who am I that v'em Adoni (the mother of my Lord) should come to me? As soon as I heard the sound of your voice, the babe in my womb leapt for joy!"

"Blessed is she believing. All those things told her by Adonai will be fulfilled!"

At Elizabeth's embrace, reality strikes home and Mary, filled with the Holy Spirit, cries out:

> "My soul magnifies Adonai, and my spirit rejoices in 'El Yesa'i (God my Savior), for he looked upon the humble state of his servant-girl. Just imagine; from now on, all generations will call me blessed!"

> "Elohim has done great things for me. Holy is his name!"

> "His mercy is to generations of generations of those who fear him!"

> "He has performed mighty deeds with his arm and routed the secretly proud."

> "He brought down rulers from their thrones and exulted the humble."
>
> "He filled the hungry with good things and sent the rich away empty."
>
> "He has helped his servant Isra'el, never forgetting the mercy, which he promised to 'avoteinu …to Avraham, and to his seed forever!"

We assume it fell to Joseph to take little Mary and 'an explanation' back to his father in law. Mary had decided to stay on with Elizabeth for what turned out to be three whole months …so magnetic was the bond between them, and so insistent was Elizabeth that she should stay[11].

After Mary had returned home, the time came for Elizabeth to give birth, and she gave birth to a son.

Her neighbors and relatives all rejoiced with her when they heard what great mercy the Lord had displayed toward her.

On the eighth day, when they came to circumcise the child, they were going to call him Zacharias after his father. But Elizabeth said, "No. He

---

11   It was customary that a woman should do no work for the first three months of pregnancy.

must be called Yochanan!" And they said to her, "None of your dod are called by that name."

And they made signs to his father about what he wanted him called. He asked for a tablet and wrote: "His name is Yochanan." And they were all astonished.

At once, Zechariah's power of speech returned and he began to speak in praise of God.

Fear came on all those living around them, and all these matters were being talked about in all the hill country of Judea. All who heard them kept them in mind, saying, "What then will this child become? For the hand of the Lord was certainly with him."

And his father Zechariah was filled with the Holy Spirit, and prophesied:

> "Praised be Adonai, the Elohim of Yisra'el,
>
> for he has visited us and made a ransom to liberate his people.
>
> He has raised up a horn of salvation for us in the house of his servant, David.
>
> It is just as he said by the mouth of his holy prophets from the beginning;

Salvation from our enemies, and from the hand of all who hate us;

to show mercy toward our 'av, and to remember his holy covenant;

the oath which he swore to Avraham avinu.

To grant us that we, being rescued from the hand of our enemies, might serve him without fear, in holiness and righteousness before him all our days!

And you, child, will be called the prophet of Ha'Elyon;

for you will go before Adonai to prepare his ways...

To give his people the knowledge of salvation by the forgiveness of their sins,

because of the tender mercy of Eloheinu, with which the Sunrise from Heaven will visit us,

to shine upon those who sit in darkness and the shadow of death...

to guide our feet into the way of peace."

The child grew and became strong in spirit and lived in the desert until the day of his public appearance to Israel.

※ ※ ※ ※ ※

Mary arrives home less than a week before John's birth and the 'Festival of Spring'; Passover …

"Oh, Bati[12], we've missed you so much!" Mary and her mother embrace as if they had been apart for years…

"My, but you look well. Your face is more beautiful to my eyes than ever I can remember!"

"Oh 'Imi; really … It's only been a few short months!"

"Short for you maybe, but your 'av and I have been so worried for you."

"I am perfectly alright 'Em. Didn't Yosef give you my message?"

"Yes, of course, but we just didn't expect you to be gone so long. How is your doda?"

"She is perfectly alright. She's having a baby."

"Yes, I gathered that from the message Yosef brought back. So it's really true then?"

---

12 Bati: My Daughter

"Yes. It will be any day now, perhaps even today. Salome is with her even now to deliver."

"That's amazing! They are too old ...Both of them."

"With Adonai, 'Imi, nothing is impossible."

Just then, Mary's father hobbles out from the house...

"Miryam; Bati! You're just in time to help with preparations for Pesach. We've invited the neighbors to join us as Barukh and your brothers have gone up to Yerushalayim for the feast. Today I must bring home a lamb ...and the house is not yet set in order."

"I will bring the lamb 'avi."

"It's not far," he says, leaning on his staff.

"You can take your 'ahot with you. It's in the manger behind the house of Salmai. But later; come ... tell us all the news of Z'kharyah and Elisheva. We got this strange story from Yosef..."

"'Avi; it's true ...They're having a son!"

"Oh, a son now is it?! How can you be so sure it will be a boy?"

"The angel, Gavri'el, appeared to Z'kharyah in the Temple and told him so before the child was even conceived!"

Mary's heart was pounding. Would she dare tell her father everything?

"Who told you this?"

"Doda Elisheva told me herself. She even showed me Z'kharyah's drawing of Gavri'el."

"Well, it certainly is a miracle. They've been childless for as long as I can remember."

"Your stay with them certainly hasn't done you any harm. You're looking absolutely glorious. They must have fed you on milk and honey, did they?"

"'Avi; Adonai has surrounded me with his grace…"

"That, my little sweetheart, is plain to see. You'd better rest up a bit before you go to Salmai's for the lamb. I hope you won't have to carry it."

"That's alright 'Avi. I don't mind carrying a little lamb."

> *"That's alright 'Avi. I don't mind carrying a little lamb."*

That afternoon, Mary carries in a perfect little lamb, freshly cleaned and lovingly dried with a towel. With a loving kiss, she places it in the living room, and sits down beside it for comfort as it adjusts to its new surrounds.

"I will call you 'Anwa, (meekness) for you are the meekest little lamb I have ever met."

"'Imi; what are you cooking? It smells wonderful!"

"I'm baking bread ... Some for us, and some to sell at the market in the morning. Your 'av says it's better than selling the surplus chametz to some Gentile for half price. Only four days now to Erev Pesach you know."

"Yes ... I know," says Mary, hugging ''Anwa' to her cheek as tears begin to well up in her eyes.

Her mother, hearing Mary's silence, closes the oven and walks in...

"You never learn, do you girl."

"Miryam; you're a betrothed woman now. You must learn to restrain yourself for the sake of custom ...and you should not be sitting like that on the floor either."

"Yes 'Imi. I just can't help the way I feel. Are we not meant to feel remorse for the life of the lamb? Is its life not forfeit in place of ours?"

"Oh Bati, sometimes I wonder why I even bother trying. Come and help me knead the last batch of dough. Be careful not to spill any yeast. It will not go unnoticed by your 'av you know."

Mary's rising, just a little slower than usual, is glanced by her mother out of the corner of her eye as she returns to the kitchen…

"You must be feeling tired. It's been a big day for you."

"Yes. It was an early start, and such a long walk. I've been feeling like just going to bed all afternoon."

"Well, this won't take long …then you might have time for a short nap before supper."

That evening, Mary slept so soundly that her mother could not wake her at supper time. This and many other little things known only to watchful mothers caused her to become … more than concerned … perhaps even a little 'suspicious', of Mary's state. But it was Pesach …so, in the words of her husband, 'all such matters shall therefore be set aside until after the final day of observance is complete.'

Three mornings later, Mary is not feeling well. After barely tasting her breakfast, she returns to her room, for she knows that 'Anwa will be slain. She does not want to see it, yet the images of red blood on white wool are vivid in her memory from Passovers gone by.

In the afternoon, as she helps her mother prepare the Seder, she tries to put it out of her mind

...but of course, on such an occasion as this, this is just impossible.

As evening approaches, it is time for 'Bedikat Chametz'; the search for the leaven. This they do every year throughout the house under the supervision of Mary's father, who also pronounces the blessing. Her mother holds a candle, Mary, a wooden spoon and her little sister wields a feather. Together, the four of them begin to search every corner...

"Blessed are you Adonai Eloheinu, who has set us apart with his commandments, and commanded us to remove the Chametz."

As they search together, Mary's father breaks the customary silence to just drop a comment:

"You know Miryam, chametz is really just a sign. It speaks of the evil impulses of the heart which arouse people to do evil deeds. When we search for the chametz, we should really search our own deeds and hearts."

"Yes 'Avi, you have taught us this from an early age. Why do you remind me again now?"

Mary's mother looks up, and is about to respond, but Heli, resting one hand on her mother's shoulder, replies; "Adonai has commanded that we should teach his precepts to our children and to our children's children. This is why I never grow tired of explaining to you the story." But in the light of the candle, Mary can see in her mother's eyes that she knows.

Mary feels feint, yet they continue the search, carefully checking every part of the house. In the end, they have half a spoonful of crumbs and one piece of crust.

The crumbs, the spoon, the candle and the crust all go into a bag to be burned.

Heli, looking at Mary, pronounces his usual disclaimer:

"All chametz which is in my house, which I have not found, and of which I am unaware shall be considered void and owner-less, like the dust of the earth!"

A knock at the door says that the neighbors have arrived. Her parents greet the guests, and Mary, holding back tears, busies herself with laying the rugs and cushions around the table. It is time to begin the Seder.

The atmosphere is lively, and Mary finds relief from her fears in the company of the guests.

Her mother slips out to the kitchen, returning with a small lamp. Everyone turns to watch her bringing the light, as a woman does on nights such as this.

She carefully lights the candles, then placing the lamp on the table, she covers her eyes with her hands as is the custom, and pronounces the blessing:

"Blessed are you Adonai Eloheinu, King of the universe, who has set us apart by his Torah, and in whose name we light the festival lights."

As she removes her hand, she wipes a tear; something entirely foreign to the traditions of that night ...and then fixes it with a smile.

Raising an eyebrow and nodding to Mary, her father gives the signal to pour the first cup...

Sitting up, he reminds them of the cup and pronounces the blessing:

"Therefore, say to the ben-Yisra'el, I am Adonai, and I will bring you out from under the burdens of Misrayim, and will deliver you from their slavery. And I will redeem you with an outstretched arm and with great judgments."

"Blessed are you, Adonai Eloheinu, king of the universe, creator of the fruit of the vine."

"Blessed are you, Adonai; you hallow the festive seasons."

"Amen! Amen!" comes the chorus of response as they all drink the cup of 'the bringing out from'; 'the cup of the setting apart'.

Mary brings the water, towel over one arm. She pours it carefully over the hands of each into a bowl; beginning with her father, then the guests as was their custom…

Taking a sprig of fresh parsley, Heli exhorts the family: "Let us dip the karpaz in salt water and be reminded of the new life that came out of the suffering in Misrayim."

Dipping, they all pronounce the blessing:

"Blessed are you, Adonai Eloheinu, king of the universe, creator of the fruit of the ground.

Mary's mother gets up and brings the matzah, the maror (bitter herb dip) and the haroset. Mary pours the wine; the second cup; 'the cup of redemption'…

"…And the blood shall be a sign to you on your houses. I will see the blood, and I will pass over you. You shall not be touched when I strike the land of Misrayim. And the day shall be a memorial for you. You shall celebrate it as a feast to Adonai, for all your generations. You shall celebrate it as a law forever. Blessed are you, Adonai Eloheinu,

King of the universe, creator of the fruit of the vine."

"Amen! Amen!"

After the wine, when the conversation finds a lull, at a nod from her father, Mary once more washes the hands of the guests with bowl and pitcher and towel… Heli, taking the matzah; blessing, he breaks it …passing it around at the "Amen".

After the matzah, Mary and her mother bring the pesah; the whole roast lamb …and place it on the table.

To the hungry souls reclining there, the aroma of satisfaction is overwhelming.

Together they all pronounce the blessing:

"Blessed are you, Adonai Eloheinu, king of the universe, who set us apart by your commandments and commanded us to eat the pesah."

The feast begins with a cheer and laughter. Mary immediately begins to refill everyone's cup…

Their neighbor, Sarai, compliments her on her appearance:

"My, but you are looking beautiful tonight Miryam. Your stay with your doda didn't do you any harm, did it! I do believe you've even put on a little weight since you've been away."

Embarrassed, Mary glances across to her mother, who has obviously been listening, for their eyes meet. Looking back to Sarai, she finds her glancing at her mother. It is too much for Mary. She places the wine down, turns, and to the bewilderment of the guests, runs up the stairs; crying, leaving them to question each other and apologize to their hearts content.

Mary's mother begins to rise up, but Heli restrains her…

"Later, wife; give her time to settle down. Pesach is a festive occasion. It is holy to Adonai."

Baruch's daughter, who is around the same age as Mary, gets up… "I'll go," she says, heading for the stairs.

At the end of the meal, after the table had been mostly cleared and her mother was washing the hands, Mary and Elisha come back down the stairs and take their places at the table…

"We saved you girls some lamb. We will wait for you to eat before we all drink from the 'Cup of Redemption'."

"The Lamb is in my heart, 'Avi, and I'm already satisfied …but I will eat just a little if it pleases you that I should eat."

> *"The Lamb is in my heart, 'Avi, and I'm already satisfied."*

"...If it pleases me?! Adonai, blessed be his name, has commanded that we should eat!"

She takes a morsel, dips it, and swallows hard, but she cannot get the images of red on white out of her mind. Her friend, Elisha, has no such problem.

The silence at the table is stifling. Elisha's mother takes up the towel and the bowl for the two girls, and Heli continues by quoting a scripture that had been fresh on his mind that day:

"In the words of the prophet, Mal'akhi: 'Remember the Torah of Moshe my servant, which I commanded him in Horev for all Yisra'el.' Adonai, blessed be his name, also said at that time: 'Look, I am sending you Eliyahu the prophet, before the coming of the great and terrible day of Adonai. He shall turn the hearts of the 'av to their ben, and the hearts of the ben to their 'av, that I not come and strike the land with utter destruction."

Heli sits up...

"Come; let us say the blessing together."

"Blessed be HaShem from this time forth and forever!"

Heli leads on…

"Let us bless Eloheinu, of whose food we have eaten, and through whose goodness we live."

"Blessed be Eloheinu, of whose food we have eaten, and by whose goodness we live!"

Taking the cup, Heli finishes…

"Blessed are you, Adonai Eloheinu, king of the universe, who in mercy and compassion gives bread to all flesh; for your mercy is everlasting. May food never fail us, for your great name's sake."

"Blessed are you, Adonai, who feeds and sustains all, and does good to all. We thank you because you brought us from the land of Misrayim, out of the house of slaves, to a good land; we thank you for your life, grace and mercy. We thank you at all times, forever. As it is said: 'When you have eaten and are satisfied, praise Adonai Eloheinu for the good land he has given you. Blessed are you, Adonai, for the land and for the food."

"Blessed are you Adonai Eloheinu, King of the universe, creator of the fruit of the vine."

"Amen! Amen!"

Heli drinks of 'Redemption', and passes his cup around for all to share.

Mary's mother immediately begins filling the fourth cup; the 'Cup of Acceptance'. When she finally gets to Mary, there are tears in her eyes. She wraps a comforting arm around her daughter as she pours the cup, then, as is the custom, her daughter pours for her. Her hand trembles as Mary pours the wine. Mary steadies it with a touch, and they embrace, cups in hand, bringing a warm response from the guests.

Mary and her mother recline together and everyone places their cup on the table while Heli chants the 'Hallel', stirring them to respond in place along the way as was his custom…

> *"Servants of Adonai, give praise! Give praise to the name of Adonai! Blessed be the name of Adonai from this moment on and forever!"*
>
> *He raises the poor from the dust, lifts the needy from the rubbish heap, in order to give him a place among princes, among the princes of his people.*
>
> *He causes the childless woman to live at home happily as a mother of children.*

Tremble, earth, at the presence of the Lord, at the presence of the God of Ya'akov, who turned the rock into a pool of water, flint into flowing spring.

I will call on him as long as I live.

The chords of death were all around me, Sh'ol's constrictions held me fast; I was finding only distress and anguish.

But I called on the name of Adonai; "Please, Adonai! Save me!"

How can I repay Adonai for all his generous dealings with me?

I will raise the cup of salvation and call on the name of Adonai…

Oh, Adonai! I am your slave; I am your slave, the son of your slave-girl; you have removed my fetters.

I will offer a sacrifice of thanks to you and I will call on the name of Adonai.

Praise Adonai, all you nations!

Worship him, all you peoples!

For his grace has overcome us, and Adonai's truth continues forever.

> *Yah is my strength and my song, and he has become my salvation.*
>
> *I will not die; no, I will live and proclaim the great deeds of Yah!*
>
> *The very rock that the builders rejected has become the cornerstone!*
>
> *Blessed is he who comes in the name of Adonai…"*

(CJB Hallel Extracts)

With cup in hand, Heli pronounces the benediction:

"Blessed are you, Adonai Eloheinu, king of the universe, who redeemed us and redeemed 'avoteinu from Misrayim."

"Blessed are you, Adonai Eloheinu, King of the universe, creator of the fruit of the vine."

"Amen! Amen!"

…And so ended the Pesach Seder that year for the houses of Heli and Baruch in Nazareth of Galilee.

"…when …Mary had been betrothed to Joseph, before they came together she was found to be with child…" (Matthew 1:18 Extract NASU)

✻ ✻ ✻ ✻ ✻

The Gates of the Kingdom

~

A story of seed-time and harvest, of sprouting and blossoming, of bearing fruit with seed unto the fullness ... A Kingdom sown, a Kingdom reaped, a glorious Bride without spot or wrinkle, a matchless gift from a Father to a Son; bone of His bone and flesh of His flesh.

Heritage Series

The Little Gate of the Great King

Part 3

...And so the rumor spread in Nazareth in those days which would one day come back to the ears of the One hidden that night in Mary's womb. It would prompt unspoken thoughts in many minds and the vehement accusation lying implicitly obvious in the words of the Pharisees:

"Where is your father?! We are not illegitimate children[13]; we have one father; God himself!"

Of course, to Joseph's ears, the news he heard from his father, Jacob, was absolutely devastating. But God did not leave him in his anguish. Mary's prayers by the lamp at her window each night brought him into that surrounding grace which was covering her.

God sent Joseph an angel in a dream, saying, 'Joseph, son of David, do not be afraid to take Mary as your wife. For that which is in her is generated by the Holy Spirit. She will bear a son, and you shall call His name Jesus, for He shall save His people from their sins.

All this happened to fulfill that which was spoken by the Lord through the prophet, saying, Behold! ...The virgin will conceive and will bear a son, and they will call His name Emmanuel; 'God with us'.'

Late that very night, Joseph did as the angel of the Lord commanded him. He came for his wife, and found the lamp still burning in the window, and his virgin bride ready for his coming ...yet with child.

---

13 See John 8:41

Shavuot[14] came and went like a shadow for Mary, who kept away from the public eye, just as Elizabeth had done. Her relationship with Joseph flourished, for it was entirely built upon believing. They believed one another because they believed God, and because of the Name. Gabriel had given to them both the same name …the name; 'Yeshua'.

And so their love grew and grew without any union in the flesh. Joseph just put such thoughts out of his mind, for the presence of the Lord had made them to vanish.

One evening, after the meal, Joseph is reclining, his head upon Mary's lap, his right foot upon his left knee. Mary is combing the sawdust out of his hair…

"Those Romans are painful. They ordered two more sets of stocks today, but the price they pay is less than what the timber is worth let alone the work I must do on it. If it weren't for the timber I salvaged off Shaarim's old barn, I'd be working for less than nothing!"

"That's alright though. The new door for the synagogue will fetch a better rate. I went and measured it up today. El'azar says that the Romans are holding a census; something to do with Augusts' birthday. They're sending a special Legate to oversee the

---

14 Shavuot: Feast of Weeks; Pentecost

whole of Syria. There's so much trouble in the land, Saturnius is apparently hard pressed just enforcing his rule."

"When will this be?"

"I'm not sure. El'azar said that the Sanhedrin would almost certainly advise the new Hegemon when he arrives, to send everyone to the towns of their 'avot …That's where they keep all the ancestral records you know."

"El'azar was in a bit of a fluster about getting the records for Natzeret up to date. I think it also explains the new door. They want to admit people one at a time for the census.

"You will have to go to Beit-Lekhem!"

"It's possible. We'll wait and see."

"Will I have to register too?"

"As far as I know. El'azar said; everybody. Don't worry. I won't leave you behind."

"There is one small detail you should try not to forget about my love."

"Oh… What's that?"

"Just look at me Yosef!"

Joseph cracks a mischievous grin… "I was only joking." he says, knowing that some swift reaction would surely follow.

"'Plenty of midwives in Natzaret,' you say! Yosef; I want Salome. I want to see her before Shavat. I won't be going anywhere without Salome."

"Consider it done my dove. If I'm late home tomorrow, you know where I'll be. I must still rough out those stocks you know."

"Good. At last we're together on this. Now I just wish I could go with you. Make sure you give my love to Elisheva and Z'kharyah …And bring me back news of baby Yochanan."

"Yes, I would like to see what manner of child is announced by an angel; Gavri'el, no less! And I am very interested in that drawing of Z'kharyah's."

"You're not supposed to know about that, don't forget."

"Don't worry, I will be discrete."

As it turned out, the governor for the census, one Publius Sulpicius Quirinus, acting on advice from the Sanhedrin, set the registration for Bethlehem right on the date that Mary was due.

The news looked very grim for anyone who failed to register for such failure implied a refusal of allegiance to Augustus …and to Rome.

It took them over a week to get there, with Salome's concern obviously mounting all the way. They finally arrived on the very last morning for registration. They went straight to the synagogue to register.

All afternoon they tried their relatives for a place to stay, but in the end, they found that there was not even room for them at the inn!

The Feast of Trumpets was about to begin just a short walk away in Jerusalem, and, apart from the census, Bethlehem had always absorbed the overflow from the feasts. Every last option was full, except for one; the manger …The manger of Bethlehem.

One ram and seven perfect yearling lambs had just vacated the premises, heading up to Jerusalem for the Feast. The rest of the 'Sacrificial Flock' were out in the fields that afternoon. And so it was that a place was made for the Little Lamb of God to enter this dark world.

Joseph shoveled and swept out the dung, made a bed for Mary from the left-over straw, and Salome cleaned and lined a feeding trough. Together, they carried it in and placed it alongside of Mary, for the birth pains had already begun.

Salome prepared the swaddling cloth and busied herself with all the preparations of a skilled midwife. Joseph had no idea what to do. When the waters burst, there was blood!

> *When the waters burst, there was blood!* [15]

At just a look from Salome, Joseph headed for the door, his head spinning.

He sat down, breathing deep the fresh evening air, listening to Mary's pain.

When he looked up, the sun was just dipping into the haze of the horizon. Some stars and the new moon had become visible in the west. There was something mesmerizing about the scene…

Suddenly; the sound of a shofars; Rosh Hashanah …the New Year had just begun!

Looking north, he could see the glow of the great signal fire on the Mount of Olives. He remembered how every year it lit up the east gate and the temple on this night.

From the walls of that city, and in the temple itself, trumpets would be sounding into the night,

---

15 See 1 John 5:6

as if to herald the coming of a great king, for this was their custom …a commandment from God Himself. It made him wonder at the place he stood, for this very night celebrated not only the birth of his forefather, Isaac, but also that day when God created Adam. According to the traditions of his forefathers, not only his own people, but the whole race of man was begotten of God on this day. 'What manner of child was this breaking out from Mary's womb?'

> …the whole race of man was begotten of God on this day. 'What manner of child was this breaking out from Mary's womb?'

The thought floated across his mind, '…and the best you could provide was a manger!' until he remembered God's sovereignty.

※ ※ ※ ※ ※

That signal fire was but the first in a chain that skipped across to Mount Gilboa on the east, then right across the Desert of Aram to Babylon, where the faithful waited for confirmation to come from Jerusalem that that thin crescent they could see in the western sky was in fact the new moon; it was officially New Year …and time to sound the shofar…

From the 'Astronomer's Turret' on the wall of Babylon, two magi of the eastern school looked up from that fire into the western sky…

"Anyone can see that it is a new moon tonight. What's the point of that fire my dod?"

"It is for those who cannot tell the times and the seasons my young neked (nephew) …And for dark nights when God hides the heavens from the eyes of men."

"What are you looking at?"

"A virgin."

"**Where!?**" (The shofars of the synagogues begin to sound throughout the city…)

"I thought that might catch your attention. Look… right there above the moon; Virgo … clothed in the sun, with the moon under her feet. This is a sign that we've been waiting for for many generations …the Virgin gives birth! It's just as Belt'shatzar taught, and this is the very year which he calculated. If it is true, then there will be another sign. We had better call the brothers. This could be awesome."

"Our eyes shall know no sleep tonight. This night, my nekhed, we shall all watch and wait."

"Wait for what? What shall be the second sign?"

"I'll explain later. Run quickly. Tell Aden to sound the gong in the courtyard. All the 'ashshawph must come quickly or they'll miss the sign of the Virgin."

❉ ❉ ❉ ❉ ❉

Between Bethlehem and Jerusalem lies the narrow Plain of the Rephaim. This is the place where the temple flocks are grazed. This night, the shepherds will camp together, for it is a night of celebration; a night for wishing each other the blessing of the New Year…

At dusk they share a meal around the fire, and at the rising of the new moon, they watch for the great signal fire on the mountain. As the stars begin to shine, the golden glow appears. One has a ram's horn. He sounds it into the night air to the cheers of all. Rising up, they each, in turn, embrace, pronouncing the blessing over and over, brother to brother as they go…

"May you be inscribed in God's book for life eternal. May you behold the beauty of Adonai and be remembered in his heavenly temple. May you prosper and be blessed with peace."

❉ ❉ ❉ ❉ ❉

Joseph winced as Mary cried out …Then, the sound of the baby crying. He dashes in…

"Are they alright?!" he blurts out to Salome as she gently wipes the newborn clean.

Gently wrapping the holy babe, she replies, "Yes; Look," rising with the child in her arms. Coming close, she passes him to Joseph, who is grinning from ear to ear …and trembling.

Kneeling beside Mary, he brings the new born Son of God beside his mother where they can see him together. Heaven's eyelids open, dark eyes all starry in the soft light of the lamp… He looks around … and grins, revealing dimples that would accompany him all his days.

…And so his first conquest was made; the heart of Joseph, son of David, carpenter of Nazareth. With no resistance, no fear, no hesitation at all, he kisses the Son, handing him to Mary. Taking him in her arms, she does exactly the same thing …and after the conquest; a yawn.

❋ ❋ ❋ ❋ ❋

Out in the fields, the shepherds return from their rounds of the herds and sit together around the fire…

"'Ah, what a glorious night", says Benjamin, lying flat on his back and gazing up at the stars.

"Yeah, I'd rather be out here on a night like this than back in town …even if it is Rosh Hashanah."

"Yerushalayim'll be a rowdy place t'night. Trumpets, feastin', dancin' even …But you're right, I kind of like these fields too. The stars seem so close t'night, you could just about reach out 'n touch 'em."

"Yeah, and we don't have to dress up and pretend to be someone special neither," adds Neriah. "…Can't imagine you lot dressin' up anyway. Yous wouldn't know what to do in a set a fine clothes. I dressed up only once in my life; for my bar-mitzvah. On that big occasion, 'Avi even made me wear his turb'n," he says, laughter echoing around the fire.

"What is that!" exclaims Benjamin, as everyone looks up toward his gaze.

They all watch frozen and dumbstruck as a brilliant star flares into blinding light …towards them! They are still looking up at where it had been when 'it' arrives.

Glorious light floods their whole field, and right there, beside their light-less burning firewood, an angel of God; awesome in appearance and radiant with glory!

"Do not fear. For behold, I proclaim good news to you; a great joy which will be to all people. Today a Saviour, Adonai Ha Mashiach, was born to you in the city of David. And this shall be a sign to you: You will find a babe, wrapped and lying in the manger."

Suddenly there appeared myriads of heavenly beings, praising God and saying, 'Glory to God in the highest … peace on earth and good will among men!'

Their rapturous praise went on and on until the shepherds themselves abandoned their fears and joined in with the heavenly host.

When the myriads of light finally vanished from their sight, the brightest of all nights turned to deep blackness. Except for the flames of their fire which had again become visible, they'd have utterly lost all direction. But they didn't care… They were still praising and jumping and hugging one another like men in a dream.

And so it was that the sacrificial flocks were abandoned that night by their shepherds at the coming of the Little Lamb of God.

> *And so it was that the sacrificial flocks were abandoned that night by their shepherds at the coming of the Little Lamb of God.*

They went straight to the manger of Bethlehem, and found the baby, just as the angel said they would.

It was a sight more wondrous even than the myriads, for, although they had seen many births in that manger, these had all been lambs …and now this one who was the Saviour, Adonai Ha Mashiach himself, lying there in a feeding trough on a bed of straw …wrapped in swaddling clothes! The 'Great One', the Saviour; the Messiah … wrapped in swaddling clothes!

They bowed down in adoration and wept for joy. They had seen God's deliverance. It answered to the deepest longings of their hearts as no mighty king on any great and glorious throne could ever do. They were very familiar with 'swaddling clothes', for they had been struggling against their bondages all their lives. Now comes their savior, overwhelmingly free and full of joy …not in a palace, but in their manger …not ruling aloof from their struggles, but wrapped in the confines of swaddling clothes! …bright eyes, a gorgeous grin and dimples!

Unable to contain their joy, they spread the news all over town. For a season, it became Bethlehem's best kept secret …A child had been born amongst them to rule on David's throne.

Because of the shepherd's report, the elders of Bethlehem were as excited as children at a birthday party. Within a few short days, they would be urging the 'Royal Family' to stay. They would even offer them a house …an offer which Joseph and Mary would gladly accept.

❆ ❆ ❆ ❆ ❆

The observation platform of the 'Astronomer's Turret' is crowded out with all the magi and their apprentices. There is hardly room to move.

Ghina picks his way through the brothers who are sprawled out all over the platform. He notices that some have dropped off to sleep. Most are watching …some talking in hushed tones. Finally he reaches his uncle, Gaspar, who is leaning back against the outer wall…

"Dod …What will this scepter that shall rise out of Isra'el look like? Will it be a long line of stars, or just a single star?"

"It could be a single star, for the words of the prophecy are that 'a star will come out of Jacob; a scepter will rise out of Isra'el'."

"The Great Belt'shatzar[16] taught that this king would come from the tribe of Judah, whose symbol is 'aRi, the lion."

---

16 Belt'shatzar: Daniel

"So that's why you're watching the east. Your waiting for 'aRi to rise."

"Should we not tell the brothers ... They're searching the whole sky?!"

"My young neked, all the 'ashshawph have received the same teaching. We shall wait and see who shall be first to recognize the sign."

Two older men approach, picking their way along the wall with many eyes following their movement... Balthazar and Melchior are definitely senior among the Magi...

"'Ah, it is almost time." says Balthazar, "Should we not tell the brothers?"

"I'm a bit worried that the bragging may be a bit much to bear if Bashaa, or Apuulluunideeszu, should happen to spot it first."

"Oh no; Heaven forbid ...Not Apuulluunideeszu! His turban would become totally inadequate."

"I thought we might just point it out when it begins to become visible."

"Yes. Good idea! Ghina, you had better get our sarat[17] to come over here. Just quietly... Wake the sleeping ones, but don't make a fuss."

---

17 sarat: apprentices

Ghina quietly moves about passing the message and all eyes turn to the gathering of apprentices at the wall. Balthazar speaks in hushed tones to about forty young men who immediately all turn to the eastern sky…

"What is the sign beginning to rise? You can just see half of it now. Who can name the sign?"

"It is 'aRi," says Ubar.

"Yes, now watch the feet."

As Leo rises, the most brilliant star appears at his feet. The gasp at the breathtaking spectacle is audible as they all start to point. The words 'Sharu' and 'scepter' come mingled with the excited gabble breaking the still of the night air.

Apuulluunideeszu steps up on the catapult ramp and makes the announcement: "A great king has been born this night! May history record that it was I, the great Apuulluunideeszu, who first interpreted the sign!"

Ignoring the cheers of Apuulluunideeszu's apprentices, Melchior quietly poses another question…

"What did Belt'shatzar call Sharu?"

Whispers all around fail to produce any answer, and at length, Melchior answers his own question…

"It is called 'Melech', which means king. But it is not just 'Melech'. Watch carefully…"

"There are two stars! They're moving apart!"

More excitement reverberates through the assembled magi. "What does it mean? Are there two kings? Is one Babylonian and the other Roman? Will Babylon separate from Rome? When will these things happen?"

Melchior quietly poses the next question for his apprentices along his well contemplated line of teaching…

"And what is the name given to the star which moves?"

…for a moment; hesitation.

"It is Tzedek! …Righteousness!"

"Yes. Very good Rabi: 'Melech Tzedek; King of Righteousness' …And the prophecy? …Do any of you know the prophecy taught by Belt'shatzar which relates to this sign?"

"…'The scepter will not depart from Judah, nor the ruler's staff from between his feet, until he comes to whom it belongs and the obedience of the nations is his.'"

"Master; why then does Tzedek appear to be departing from before the feet of 'aRi?"

"I am not sure my son, but if we watch carefully, we may see other signs, for it is yet more than two hours to the sunrise."

"It shall not depart," states Gaspar, the youngest of the three, with an air of confidence.

"But Master Caspar, Tzedek is Jupiter. It never stands still."

"Watch and learn, young sarat of Melchior. Just watch and learn."

Ever so slowly, 'Tzedek' stopped in its track and returned again to 'Melech' between the feet of ''aRi', 'the Lion'. Blazing brightly in union as before, it again proclaimed the King of Righteousness, then appeared to pass on in the opposite direction! This was something that most of the magi had never seen. How could Jupiter turn around and go the other way? Even the elders were gasping in amazement at the sight.

Gasper and Balthazar were quite familiar with the habits of Jupiter, the king of planets, but this declaration in the heavens and the accuracy of Daniel's predictions had them absolutely awestruck.

"I wonder where this King of the Jews will be born," says Balthazar, eyes transfixed on the sight.

"I don't know," replies Melchior, "The Jews are scattered everywhere from here to Alexandria, to Rome, but one thing I do know; this is a very great King above all other kings. The coming of kings is declared on the earth by men with trumpets, as on this night, but what king has ever been declared by the starry host of God in the heavens?!"

"...The coming of kings is declared on the earth by men with trumpets, as on this night, but what king has ever been declared by the starry host of God in the heavens?!"

Jupiter stopped, as if it had heard Melchior's exclamation, and returned for a third union with Regiel. Together, they were so bright; brighter even than before.

This third time at their declaration, 'Melech Tzedek, King of Righteousness', the magi of Babylon all bowed their faces to the ground and paid homage to the King! At the rising of the sun, the scepter still remained before the feet of 'aRi, the lion ...the Lion of Judah!

The excitement of Babylon's magi lasted right through that day, stirred on by the constant sound of shofars proclaiming the New Year ...proclaiming the coming of the king.

* * * * *

The Gates of the Kingdom

~

A story of seed-time and harvest, of sprouting and blossoming, of bearing fruit with seed unto the fullness ... A Kingdom sown, a Kingdom reaped, a glorious Bride without spot or wrinkle, a matchless gift from a Father to a Son; bone of His bone and flesh of His flesh.

Heritage Series

The Little Gate of the Great King

Part 4

Apart from a place to stay, the elders of Bethlehem had made sure that all the arrangements were in order for their newborn king.

As the eve of the Day of Atonement approached, just before the setting sun issued in the most holy of Sabbaths; the one day of the year when the High Priest would enter into the Holy of Holies to make atonement by blood for the nation …just then did they circumcise him.

There in the Synagogue of Bethlehem, in the presence of his father, of Joseph, the priest and the elders of David's line, the real blood of atonement was seen by human eyes for the very first time! His father's eyes saw much more. They saw the sign of a covenant cut, for it was on this very day so many years before that he had cut with his people, Israel, a covenant on new tablets of stone to replace the ones they had broken. It would be a covenant neither cut in tablets of stone nor ratified with the blood of bulls and goats…

"What name shall be called upon this child?" chants the priest, the circumcision having been completed.

"His name is Yeshua," replies Joseph, quoting words deeply embedded, "for he will save his people from their sins."

The old priest is stunned by a statement that is just too unbelievable to comprehend. Even so, his hands tremble as he gives the awesome child back to 'his father'.

Twenty three days later, it is Sunday morning, and the day of 'the Redemption of the Son'. On this day, Joseph would pay the redemption price of five silver shekels for the firstborn. Acknowledging that Jesus belonged to God, he would 'redeem' his life back to the kinship of the 'Sons of Israel'.

"Yosef?"

"Yes, my dove?"

"Have you ever had the feeling that things are repeating themselves?"

"That depends ... What do you mean?"

"The town elders ... The way they are insisting on us staying, and the way they are treating us …it's almost the same as that time I went to visit Doda Elisheva and she wouldn't let me go."

"Yes, it seems that anyone who recognizes this child never wants to let him go. There is something so captivating about him. I should know. I am his first captive. Yeshua, you have won my heart! Yes you have…" he says, taking him up in his arms. "… You and those gorgeous little dimples. I'm your slave forever, and I also will never let you go. 'Aviha (your father) is so gracious to loan you to me for only five silver shekels. This day is your 'pidyon-ha-ben'. Today I will make you to be as my own."

And so he did ... And so, under law, Jesus became 'the carpenter's son' for a season.

Nine days later, it is time for their first walk up to Jerusalem...

After purchasing a pair of young doves in the market to offer for Mary's atonement, they walk across the city and enter the temple courtyard ...

"Yosef ...this temple ...it is so grand ...the people ...they are all so dressed up ...it frightens me."

"Yes, I know. What I can't understand is that the owner of this house chose you for his handmaiden knowing full well how out of place we feel here."

"There are many women here more beautiful than I."

"No my Dove, you are mistaken. There are none."

"Yosef; you are biased."

"Yes. So is Elohim. He has a strong leaning towards people who are after his own heart."

"Look; that old man has fixed his eyes on us and he's coming this way. Do you know him?"

"Not that I recall, but he seems to know us ...or is it the baby?"

"Shalom; Shalom aleikhem! I am Shim'on," says the ancient one, stretching out his hands to receive the child.

"Oh, blessed be Adonai the giver of hayyim," he proclaims with trembling voice, kissing the holy babe on the forehead, holding him up close to see with aged, teary eyes…

"And now my immutable Master, it is time to release your bond-slave in peace according to your word, for my eyes have seen your yeshu'ah which you prepared before the face of all peoples …A light for revelation to the nations and the glory of your people Yisra'el."

And blessing his incredulous parents, Simeon hands the child back to Mary…

"Behold, this one is destined for the falling and rising of many in Yisra'el and for a miraculous sign whom people will refuse. Moreover, through your soul shall pass a great sword, that the thoughts of many hearts may be revealed."

Just at that moment, a most ancient woman came on the scene …a prophetess named Anna, daughter of Phanuel of the tribe of Asher. She stayed always in the temple grounds, worshipping there night and day with much prayer and fasting. When she saw the child, taking him in her arms, she began thanking and praising God. From that time she never ceased speaking of him to all who were eagerly watching for the redemption of Jerusalem!

※ ※ ※ ※ ※

While Joseph is busy establishing a new carpentry business in Bethlehem, the magi of Babylon are studying the stars with great interest. On the 14th of Adar, as the Jews celebrate their deliverance at Purim, another sign appears as Regiel and Jupiter unite again between the feet of Leo. Again at Shavuot, the Feast of Weeks, the same thing happens. Still, they are not sure where this great king of the Jews has been born.

All of Babylon is buzzing with rumors …all kinds of rumors. Caspar, Melchior and Balthazar wait, patiently watching the heavens. Nine months have gone by. It is the evening of the 25th of Sivan…

"Ahi, will you never grow tired of watching for a sign? Eventually you will have to face the fact that we have missed it. We have no idea where he was born, so how can we possibly go to pay homage before his face?"

"Patience Caspar. The one who set the stars in their courses is not a man that he should be influenced by our impatience."

"So true ahi, yet he set them in their courses in relation to the birth of one man …Such a man we must see …And when we see him, we shall all worship before his face."

"Master Melchior! …What is that glow in the cloud over the palace?"

"It is the Morning Star my son."

"It's very bright!"

"Yes, it is the brightest of all the stars because it declares the rising of the sun."

As the cloud moves away, Babylon is lit up by the brightest star ever seen. Breathtaking in beauty, it climbs up into the eastern sky. So brilliant is its light, that it can still be seen during the day…

"Ahi, there has never been a star such as this one. The sun is well up and it is still visible," says Caspar, wiping the sweat off his brow.

"I never thought I'd see the day we'd be watching a star at high noon."

Balthazar, looking intently into the sky, shielding his eyes from the sun, at length, answers…

"It is two stars. I see two stars. Jupiter is with it, and it is leading to the west. We have a direction."

"If that other star is Jupiter, then it will be the same again tomorrow. If it is the same, that will be enough for me," says Caspar, his implication plain to all.

"Yes ahi, we shall inform the ashshawph immediately. Shall we take the sarat with us?" asks Melchior with a twinkle in his eye.

"Master; how could you say such a thing ...of course you will take us with you! Does all our training have no purpose[18]? If you leave us behind I will never forgive you!"

The three burst into laughter at the seriousness of Ghina's reaction.

Once the Council of the Magi had settled the matter, it still took three months to prepare for the expedition. Camels and supplies for 45 men plus servants and guards was quite an undertaking even in Babylon. It was a small army that eventually rode out into the western desert following that star...

* * * * *

Now after Jesus was born in Bethlehem of Judea in the days of Herod the king, magi from the east arrived in Jerusalem, saying, "Where is He who has

18 As then, still today; Jesus is the one who gives purpose and value to all things.

been born King of the Jews? For we saw His star in the east and have come to worship Him."

When Herod the king heard this, he was troubled, and all Jerusalem with him.

Gathering together all the chief priests and scribes of the people, he inquired of them where the Messiah was to be born. They said to him, "In Bethlehem of Judea; for this is what has been written by the prophet: 'and you, Bethlehem, land of Judah, are by no means least among the leaders of Judah; for out of you shall come forth a ruler who will shepherd my people Israel.'"

Then Herod secretly called the magi and determined from them the exact time the star appeared. And he sent them to Bethlehem and said, "Go and search carefully for the Child; and when you have found Him, report to me, so that I too may come and worship Him."

After hearing the king, they went their way; and the star, which they had seen in the east, went on before them until it came and stood over the place where the Child was.

When they saw the star, they rejoiced exceedingly with great joy. After coming into the house they saw the Child with Mary His mother; and they fell to the ground and worshiped Him. Then, opening their treasures, they presented to Him gifts of gold, frankincense, and myrrh. And having been warned by God in a dream not to return to Herod, the magi left for their own country by another way.

Now when they had gone, behold, an angel of the Lord appeared to Joseph in a dream and said, "Get up! Take the Child and His mother and flee to Egypt, and remain there until I tell you; for Herod is going to search for the Child to destroy Him."

So Joseph got up and took the Child and His mother while it was still night, and left for Egypt. He remained there until the death of Herod. This was to fulfill what had been spoken by the Lord through the prophet: "Out of Egypt I called my Son."

Then when Herod saw that he had been tricked by the magi, he became very enraged, and sent and slew all the male children who were in Bethlehem and all its vicinity, from two years old and under, according to the time which he had determined from the magi.

Then what had been spoken through Jeremiah the prophet was fulfilled: "A voice was heard in Ramah, weeping and great morning, Rachel weeping for her children; and she refused to be comforted; because they were no more."

But when Herod died, behold, an angel of the Lord appeared in a dream to Joseph in Egypt, and said, "Get up, take the Child and His mother, and go into the land of Israel; for those who sought the Child's life are dead."

So Joseph got up, took the Child and His mother, and came into the land of Israel. But when he heard that Archelaus was reigning over Judea in place of his father Herod, he was afraid to go there. Then after being warned by God in a dream, he left for the regions of Galilee, and came and lived in a city called Nazareth.

This was to fulfill what was spoken through the prophets: "He shall be called a Nazarene." (Matthew 2 NASU)

By Colin Baker © 2007 All rights reserved

www.colininthespirit.com

The Gates of the Kingdom

~

A story of seed-time and harvest, of sprouting and blossoming, of bearing fruit with seed unto the fullness ... A Kingdom sown, a Kingdom reaped, a glorious Bride without spot or wrinkle, a matchless gift from a Father to a Son; bone of His bone and flesh of His flesh.

Heritage Series

The Jordan Gate III

My brother, my sister, within you and I lives One who knows well His days in the gates. They were days that shifted the order of this cosmos. Come with me on an inner journey. Allow the Wiser half of your spirit, that One who keeps His peace while we are so busy; allow your Lord to speak within you, and tell of just one of those days of splendor and glory...

For the Son of Man, the day began in what had been my home town of Natzeret in the Galil, where I had grown up with Yosef, my 'em, Miryam, my 'ah, Ya'akov, Yosi, Y'hudah and Shim'on, as well as my three 'ahot…

I still see the day that I'd heard of my dod, Yochanan, immersing in the gate; immediately I sensed the strong calling of Elo'i, 'avi[19], within.

I turned my face towards Beit-'Avara[20], knowing that the old realm of Bashan lay just beyond that house.

As I committed myself to depart my flesh, my dod, those brutes of Bashan made their interests known. It was a long way to Beit-'Avara, 'the house beyond'. I clung to 'avi, my life, and stepped out onto the road.

As the Son of Man, I was about thirty years of age when 'avi called me out from my dod (beloved relatives) to the gate.

It was the time of the barley harvest. There was much joy in my fellow travelers as we walked together through whitened fields to the south of Tavor. We reached the gate of Na'im at the time of the afternoon shade. I went in and spent the evening

---

19   Elo'i, Avi: 'My God, My Father'
20   Beit-'Avara: The House Beyond (the Jordan; opposite Jerico)

with friends. They asked, 'Where are you going?' I replied, 'Yochanan is immersing at Beit-'Avara. I'm going there because 'avi has sent me.' This caused much bewilderment to my hosts, but still they received me with joy and we parted with blessings.

Half a day's walk brought me to Scythopolis, the foreign 'Decapolis' of Herod. The road went right through the center of the city.

The main street was lined on both sides with government buildings and the homes of the rich and powerful. The sun was shining, but there was no light in Scythopolis. Its slaves rode in chariots, but there was no joy on their faces. It was a busy place void of life.

Light and life walked through but nobody noticed.

It was a long way to Sal'im. I slept in the field that night alone with 'avi, admiring the stars we'd strewn across the heavens together. I woke before morning wet with the dew and harassed by mosquitoes …Full of the joy of 'avi.

I walked in strength to Sal'im for 'avi had prepared breakfast for me there!

Shabbat found me in the shadow of the mountain at Gilgal alone, but I was not alone. There I made a fire and sat with 'avi. He comforted me and I received his comfort and responded with heartfelt love.

In the morning I moved on to ascend a small, familiar hill. It was there that I'd met with Y'hoshua on that momentous morning … The morning before his stewardship of my redemption of this land. The battle was won that day when I drew my sword and struck him down with it[21].

Many people were gathered there because it was midway between Yericho and the gate. It also provided a good view of the Yarden, as fifty sons of the prophets had once discovered. This was the place where Yochanan was now baptizing.

I stood for a while in the crowd and observed. There were many wet and happy faces. Many had also come out of curiosity to hear the fiery prophet of the wilderness. Others had come in their despair, searching for hope.

His voice was loud and clear; 'Come, repent, for the Kingdom of Heaven is near!' he would call out. And the people would come. Hundreds of the lost sheep of Yisra'el were finding their hearts inclined towards my appearing. The whole climate of Yisra'el was being affected by Yochanan

---

21   The drawn sword in His hand that day was just a symbol. To see the real sword look at Revelation 1:16.

in preparation for that very next day when I would be presented by 'avi in the gate.

My heart went out to him; for there was a kingdom bond between us in spirit.

Not following my own inclination, I crossed over with the crowds following the leading of 'avi. He led me into the village of Beit-'Avara, to the house beyond that he had prepared for me. I found my welcome there.

And so, my 'ah, my 'ahot, it was in the ancient land of wild Bashan that the Son of Man knelt in prayer and laid all his human heritage upon the altar of his heart. I considered well those things that would not come up from the Yarden on the morrow.

The seed must bear the pattern for the full harvest, and you, my beloved, are my seed.

I saw lying deep within that heritage of my flesh that primordial instinct of wild Bashan called self-preservation. This always brings one to the only law that Bashan ever knew; survival of the fittest; the strongest of the flesh, the law of wild dogs and bulls and of the nations.

That night, the adversary came to me, the Son of Man, in the late watch of the night. He had a dark sword in his hand… "Where is your sword Adonai Tzva'ot?" he taunted.

"I have my sword," I calmly replied, "and I know that which I shall defend." He vanished back into his place of darkness.

In the morning I walked with 'avi to the gateway of his rest.

There assembling in the gate were thousands of witnesses, the elders of the people and Yochanan-Na-vi'el (the prophet of Elohim). I looked around and I noticed that my friends were also there. They didn't know me then, but I knew them.

I knew that all things were ready, so I immediately went down into the water with those responding to the call of 'avi in Yochanan. As I, in turn approached, our spirits leapt within us, and he said, "It is I who should be baptized by you … Do you come to me?"

I answered and said, "Allow it now, for it is fitting for us to fulfil all righteousness." And so, he allowed.

I went down into the water and there delivered up the heritage of my human birth for dissolution. Praying fervently, I came up like Malki-Tzedek having nothing but a cup and a loaf and the power of 'avi's life within. I lost nothing, but I left some things behind in the water.

....

I gave thanks to 'avi for his rest. I had entered through the gate into 'avi's rest. Little children, you must always enter into my rest before you can do my works.

In the heavens the gate was opened and I recalled that moment before creation when we settled this matter. We had agreed then that we both would pay the price. The Ruach Ha Kodesh descended as a dove, lighting upon my head. 'Avi proclaimed to me in the hearing of the witnesses and of my friends; "You are my ben, the beloved; I am delighted in you!"

I was exulted and my spirit ascendant in the revelation that I had glorified 'avi. In spirit we danced together within the glory redounding between us!

> *Little children, you must always enter into my rest before you can do my works*

....

I went up from the gate stirred mightily, sharing again in glory with 'avi …full of his life!

Returning the short distance into Beit-'Avara, I collected my mantle and dried my clothes, the spirit stirring me still. I set my face toward the wilderness of Bashan; toward the mountains of 'Avarim. That very same place where Mikha'el, my 'eved, had contended with Satan for the body of my friend Moshe.

I went out to do battle with the devil. I ate nothing, and was there forty days with the wild creatures. At the end of that time, I was hungry, and so the devil came to me. He said, "If you are Ben-Elohim, preserve your life; turn this stone into bread."

This suggestion was very similar to what 'Imi had on occasions known me to do for others. I drew my sword, and said, "It has been written; 'Man shall not live by bread alone but by every word of Elohim.'"

I glanced across to the heights of Pisgah, and as I stood again on those heights, the devil came to me and showed me all the kingdoms of this world. He said, "I will give all this authority and their glory to you because it has been delivered to me and I give it to whomever I wish. If you worship before me, all will be yours."

Drawing my sword again, I said to him, "Get behind me Satan, for it has been written, 'you shall worship Adonai Eloheinu and him only shall you serve.'"

The Devil has shifty eyes. He glanced across to the pinnacle of the temple in Yerushalayim. I went in pursuit. There on that pinnacle he said to me, "If you are Ben-Elohim, throw yourself down; for it has been written, 'He will command his angels about you, to preserve you; that on their hands they shall bear you, lest you should strike your foot against a stone.'"

Again I drew my sword, and said to him, "It has been commanded, 'You shall not tempt Adonai Eloheinu.'"

Then the devil left me and the angels of 'avi came and cared for me.

I returned in the power and the glory of the Ruach Ha Kodesh, on foot, to Beit-'Avara. Knowing that Yochanan would soon be arrested by Herod, I spent two more days there.

When he saw me walking towards him, he cried out, "Behold, the Lamb of Elohim, who takes away the sin of the world. This One is truly Ben-Elohim!"

So neither did the Messiah glorify Himself to become cohen gadol; rather, it was the One who said to him, "You are My Son; today I have become your father." Also, as he says in another place, "You are a cohen forever, to be compared with Malki-Tzedek." (Hebrews 5:5-6 JNT)

Yochanan's words stirred very deep memories within me of that time before time, when before 'avi's eyes, I became fully a lamb.

The next day, Yochanan again pointed me out to two of his disciples; "Look, the Lamb of Elohim!" he said. They began to follow me …a lamb!

I stopped and asked them what they wanted. They said, 'Rabbai, where are you staying?' so I said, 'Come and see.'

We walked together back to my lodging, which was a new room out back of a house of poverty. My hosts had prepared it for my coming. They had listened to Yochanan and believed what they heard. There was no furniture but clean fresh straw on an earthen floor.

I introduced them to my hosts, and their children. We spent the rest of the afternoon together in the fellowship of just getting acquainted.

Within the first hour, Andrew became very excited and excused himself. He dashed out and returned a short time later with his brother. I looked at him and said, "You are Shim'on bar-Yochanan; you shall be known as Kefa[22]."

The next day I was ready to leave for the Galil, but not before we went and found Philip. When I saw him, I said, "Follow me!" I knew he would. He was

---

22 Kefa: Bowing, the cupped palm of ones hand or a great arching rock (David may have written many of the Psalms in a kefa.)

from Beit-Tzaida, the home town of Andrew and Kefa.

Still, we didn't leave straight away because Philip had to go and find Natan'el. 'We've found the one that Moshe wrote about in the Torah, also the prophets,' he says, 'it's Yeshua Ben-Yosef from Natzaret!'

'Natzaret!? Can anything good come from there?' 'Come and see', he says.

When I saw Natan'el coming, I said 'Here's a true son of Yisra'el … Nothing false in him!'

Natan'el was surprised and asked, 'How do you know me?' So I told him, 'Before Philip found you, I saw you under the fig tree!'

Natan'el was stunned! 'Rabbai,' he said, 'you are Ben-Elohim! You are the King of Yisra'el!'

I couldn't but grin at his face. 'You believe all of this,' I said, 'just because I told you I saw you under the fig tree?'

Knowing that he would later gain understanding, I said to him, 'You'll see greater things than these! Truly, truly I say to you, from now on, you will see Heaven opened and the angels of Elohim ascending and descending on the Son of Man!'

This one, from now on, would dwell outside the gate in Beit-El, the house of 'avinu. He would experience the joining of heaven and earth in me, the Son of Man, for I am the door. Only then would he be able to know how I saw the fig tree. I saw it with other eyes …inner eyes …his eyes.

By Colin Baker © 2007 All rights reserved

www.colininthespirit.com

The Gates of the Kingdom

~

A story of seed-time and harvest, of sprouting and blossoming, of bearing fruit with seed unto the fullness ... A Kingdom sown, a Kingdom reaped, a glorious Bride without spot or wrinkle, a matchless gift from a Father to a Son; bone of His bone and flesh of His flesh.

Heritage Series

The Communion Gate

When some were speaking about the temple, how it was adorned with beautiful stones and gifts dedicated to God, he said, "As for these things that you see, the days will come when not one stone will be left upon another; all will be thrown down." (Luke 21:5-6 NRSV)

The season of the approach of Hanukkah had been one rough, gut-wrenching journey for the twelve. Their Lord had been accused of being illegitimate, insane and demonic.

The fact that these accusations, and the plots of jealous men had not ruffled their Master, did not help them one little bit …they were exhausted. Jesus woke very early in the morning, left his disciples sleeping, and went into the temple…

…Then came Hanukkah in Yerushalayim. It was winter, and Yeshua was walking …in Shlomo's Colonnade. (John 10:22-23 JNT extracts)

The days of the Son of Man passed quickly and the season for my baptism was almost upon me. Yet again I felt the strong desire of my 'av within me. There was this yearning for a place, a very special place; an ancient abode …the throne room of 'avi. These stones and pillars were to me more than just a relic of a by-gone era. They were in fact the last remains of the model prepared by Y'didyah[23] …a temporary dwelling place amongst the sons of men. Now, I would go to prepare an eternal dwelling place; not a model, but the fullness …not amongst the sons of men, but within them …it was time.

As I walked the Colonnade, I saw and contemplated many things …memories of events about to take place and the glory of things that would surely come, for this was the place of my second birth…

....

---

23   Y'didyah: Jedediah; Beloved of God; Solomon

'I know these steps. This is where the scoffers stood who accused me of being drunk. And this portico …yes, I remember it was from here that I answered their accusations through Shim'on Kefa. That shocked the Adversary! This is where the realization of what I had done first began to dawn on him. And those baptismal pools …that's where I first broke out, paw-rach, into the three thousand. Here, by the mouths of the Hundred and Twenty, I was born into mankind … Parthians, Medes, Elamites, Mesopotamians, Judeans, Asians, Phrygians, Pamphylians, Cyrenians, Egyptians, Libyans, Romans, Cretians, Arabians and on to the ends of the earth. Right here at Pentecost, by our indwelling, the confusion of Bavel was undone and your Kingdom has come in. Truly your will, 'avi, shall be done on Earth even as it is done in Heaven.'

''Avi, when we revealed our character, our desire, our will to Isra'el on tablets of stone, three thousand died. Here in Shlomo's Colonnade, when we came into them, bringing our character, our desire and our will inside, three thousand came to life! This is the place 'avi, where your glory burst forth and hayyim[24] became available to man. Right here his exile ended. Now he will be able to partake of hayyim and become one with us.' (ref. Genesis 3:22 and Revelation 22:2)

---

24 hayyim: life (original, plural, transcendent)

"Avi, I count the cost, but today, I also count the reward, for your glory is my reward. Your will, I choose, and desire with all my heart. Your love is high above all things, its value greater even than hayyim.'

'My ben, not all made aliyah as soon as we came into them. Even those who did still had to daily choose to will with our will and desire with our desire to taste of the fruit of our tree. As you have so desired my ben, her love shall be forever dependent on that place she gives you in her heart. Our heartache for the love of man did not end at Pentecost, but at Pentecost our heart ceased to ache alone. Our desire shall surely be fulfilled. Pentecost is our first-fruits as well as theirs.'

'Her choosing is your enthronement on this Earth 'avi, for you are always enthroned between the cherubim.'

....

"Hey! …You there!"

"It's him. We've got him this time! Surround him!"

"How long will you keep us in suspense? If you are ha Mashiach, tell us publicly."

"I told you, and you didn't believe. The works I do in the name of 'avi, these bear witness about me. The reason you don't believe is because you are not my sheep. As I already told you, my sheep hear my voice. I know them, and they follow me. To them, I give eternal life and they'll never perish, even to the age! No-one shall ever pluck them out of my hand, for 'avi who has given them to me is greater than all and no one can pluck out of 'avi's hand. I and the 'av are one!"

Incensed, they took up stones to stone him…

"I showed you many good works from 'avi. For which work of them do you stone me?"

"Not for the good works, but for blasphemy. You, being a man, make yourself Elohim!"

"Has it not been written in your Torah, 'I said, you people are elohim'? If He called those elohim to whom the word of Elohim was, and the Scripture cannot be broken, do you say of Him whom the 'av set apart to himself and sent into the world, 'You blaspheme', just because I said, I am ben Elohim?"

"If I do not do the works of 'avi, do not believe Me. But if I do, then even if you do not believe me, believe the works, that you may perceive and discover that the 'av is in me, and that I am in him."

Again they sought to seize him, but he easily went out from their hand. He took his disciples out across the Jordan to Beit-Avara, 'the house beyond', where John was at first baptizing and remained there with them.

Many came to Him and said, "Yochanan did no miraculous sign, but everything Yochanan said about this one is true. And many believed into him there…

If you love Me, keep My commandments. And I will petition the Father, and He will give you another Comforter, that He may remain with you to the age, the Spirit of Truth, whom the world cannot receive, because it does not see Him nor know Him. But you know Him for He abides with you and shall be in you. (John 14:15-17 LITV)

…If anyone loves Me, he will keep My Word, and My Father shall love him. And We will come to him and will make a dwelling place with him. (John 14:23b LITV)

By Colin Baker © 2007 All rights reserved

www.colininthespirit.com

The Gates of the Kingdom

~

A story of seed-time and harvest, of sprouting and blossoming, of bearing fruit with seed unto the fullness ... A Kingdom sown, a Kingdom reaped, a glorious Bride without spot or wrinkle, a matchless gift from a Father to a Son; bone of His bone and flesh of His flesh.

Heritage Series

The Tzion Gate

...even we heard this voice being borne out of Heaven, being with Him in the holy mountain. (2 Peter 1:18)

It is very late in the night. There is a chill in the air and, apart from the occasional yapping of dogs, the back-streets of Jerusalem have gone quiet.

Into this drowsy scene comes a great commotion. Twelve boisterous men make their way through the narrow streets to a very dark doorway.

As they approach, the door opens, light floods out, and laughter echoes around the stone walls as a man and his wife welcome them inside. Receiving a lamp from their hosts, Marcus and Mariam, they ascend the stairs to the loft…

"Watch out for that last step! There's a plank loose! Somebody show Mattityahu. We don't want to lose him on his first night."

"Well shine the lamp back this way a bit! That's better. Watch your step 'ah, that one's broken."

"This is the place; the upper room. Since Pesach (Passover), this has been our home."

Sandals are thrown into the corner and coats and mats rolled out, some of the brothers stirring up the dust to the raucous protest of the others. Eventually they are all reclined and, for a moment, there is quiet in the loft …but only for a moment …

"'Ahim[25], this has been a good day. Now we're twelve again, and it's good. I'm so glad Mattityahu has joined us."

"Yeah, amen, amen," they all agree.

"I agree with Ya'akov," says John with a big grin on his face, "today something moved. Something amazing'll happen. I can feel it coming."

---

25 'Ahim: Brothers

"Surely nothing could be more glorious than these last days with Yeshua Adonai," contributes Philip.

"I don't know," says John, "one time on the mountain; on Tavor, we saw his glory. Ya'akov and Kefa and me, we saw him."

Philip looks questioningly to Peter… "He said we should tell no-one until after his resurrection," he replied.

"Well tell us then!"

"Yeah, come on, tell us the story, we all want to know."

"Yochanan, I believe this would be a good time for the three of us to tell what we saw that night," says Peter, James nodding his approval.

Philip claps his hands together; "This'll be good!" he declares, as they all huddle in close to listen to the three.

Peter begins: "You would all remember that day in Nain, it was really the first time we'd begun to work together with Yeshua to shoulder some of the burden of his ministry …well, that's the way it seemed to us then. Looking back, I see that actually, he was preparing us for these days now."

Andrew, putting his hand to his head, interjects; "I remember," he says, and the eight all burst into rowdy laughter.

"I don't get it?" says Peter.

"No, you were climbing the mountain at the time," replies Philip, "but while you four were away, Shim'on heals this young fellow with a dislocated hip. Well, he was so excited that he threw away his crutches and hit Andrew on the head!"

"Yeah, well it wasn't a real slick operation all round, was it," Andrew confesses, "but we learnt a lot."

"Yeah, like; 'duck when Shim'on goes into action'," says Thomas to more fits of laughter from all including Andrew and Simon.

"At last we hear what you all got up to in our absence," says Peter, quite un-amazed.

"Well …it was a long way to the top of Tavor, and not much shade on those grassy slopes as you well know. Yeshua was walking in the power of the Ruach Ha Kodesh that day. We struggled to keep pace with him."

"He knew why we were climbing the mountain. We had no idea what he meant when he said that he must go up to pray, and that we should come with him. It was only afterwards that we remembered that he said we'd see his kingdom coming in power."

"That night we saw what power really is. It is not what men understand it to be. We had no idea!"

"Kefa speaks the truth," contributes John, "there is a Holy Mountain. On that night it was to Tavor, and we knew it not."

"No," confirms James, "We were all weighed down with sleep."

"On top of Tavor, there's a flat rock, like a threshing floor. Our Lord was kneeling there in prayer, but after a few short hours, we went and reclined on the grass."

"Reclined?" says John, "We lay down; all three of us!"

"Yes, but we didn't all go to sleep. Did we?" says Peter. "Actually I could hear people talking, but I thought I was dreaming. It was Moshe and Eliyahu talking with Yeshua about that very exodus which He has now accomplished for us."

"Hallelujah, glory, praise Adonai!" they all chorused together.

"Hush my 'ah, there's more. Let Kefa finish the story." says James.

"Eliyahu was saying something about the Ruach Ha Kodesh and those who would see Mashiach ascend, and there was light. When I realized that I was not dreaming, I looked up and saw them. We all looked up together."

"What did Eliyahu say?" interjects Bartholomew.

"I don't understand; something about 'two mouths'. I'm not sure what he meant."

"They were all so glorious! Yeshua's clothing had become whiter than snow in the sunshine and his face shone with the Sh'khinah of Elohim. The light was shining out from Him!"

"He took my breath away, he was so glorious. I didn't know what to say, so I said something. Do you remember what I said Ya'akov?"

"You said 'Lord it is good that we are here, if you want, I will make three shelters,' but I don't think you knew what you were saying. You were speaking completely out of place."

"Yes, I felt ashamed and naked in the light of their holiness, and something in me must have wanted to cover up."

"But even as I spoke, a brilliant white cloud enveloped us and Elohim the true 'av of all things spoke. He said; 'This is my beloved son, in whom I am fully satisfied. Listen to him!'"

John continues; "When we heard that voice, we all cast ourselves prostrate on the ground, our eyes closed and trembling. Then Yeshua came and touched us, we looked up and it was all over. Moshe and Eliyahu were gone, and we were alone again with Yeshua."

"We worshiped him."

"We worshiped him ...and ... He told us not to tell anyone until after his death and resurrection."

"When we came down the mountain in the morning I was so overwhelmed by his glory that my legs had turned to jelly and I had difficulty walking."

"Yes, it was the same for all three of us."

"Now he's reigning both in us and on high in that same glory we saw on the mountain!"

"Come; let's worship the Lord in the beauty of his holiness!"

....

Yea, I have set My king on my holy mount on Zion.

I will declare concerning the statute of Jehovah: He said to Me, You are My Son, today I have begotten You.

Ask of Me, and I will give the nations as Your inheritance; and the uttermost parts of the earth as

Your possession. You shall break them with a rod of iron; You shall dash them in pieces like a potter's vessel.

Now then, be wise, O kings; be taught O judges of the earth: Serve Jehovah with fear; yea rejoice with trembling.

Kiss the Son, lest He be angry, and you perish from the way, when His wrath is kindled but a little.

O the blessings of all who are fleeing to Him for refuge! (Psalm 2:6-12 LITV)

By Colin Baker © 2012 All rights reserved

www.colininthespirit.com

Other Books by Colin Baker

from The Voice Series:

The Voice in Galatians

The Voice in Thessalonians

The Voice in 1 Corinthians

...with more to come.

from The Gates of the Kingdom Series:

The Gates of the Kingdom Part 1

The Gates of the Kingdom Part 2

The Little Gate of the Great King

...with more to come.

These titles and many more are available in PDF, ePub and Audio format for Laptop, Tablet and Mobile devices from
www.colininthespirit.com

❈ ❈ ❈ ❈ ❈

Other Copyright

NASU Scripture quotations taken from the New American Standard Bible® Copyright © 1960, 1962, 1963, 1968, 1971, 1972, 1973, 1975, 1977, 1995 by The Lockman Foundation

Used by permission. www.Lockman.org

(NASU Indicates the New American Standard Bible Updated Edition)

(CJB / JNT) Indicates that the scripture was taken from the Complete Jewish Bible / Jewish New Testament Copyright © 1979 by David H Stern

Published by Jewish New Testament Publications, Inc. www.messianicjewish.net/jntp

Distributed by Messianic Jewish Resources.

LITV Scripture taken from the Literal Translation of the Holy Bible Copyright © 1962 - 1998 by Jay P. Green, Sr.

Used by permission of the copyright holder.

www.SpiritAndTruth.org

* * * * *

About the Author

Colin Baker lives in Australia's Northern Territory in the remote Aboriginal Homeland Community of Gäwa.

Gäwa is a name well loved. It's origins are Macassan. It means 'Land of the King'.

His experience at Gäwa has been one of pioneering and gate-keeping, perseverance, patience and overcoming.

He is committed to the glory of God as is reflected in his vision to facilitate an embracing of the Gospel of the Glory by God's people.

His mandate is pictured in Ezekiel chapter one when viewed in the light of the fact that 'movement in the Spiritual Realm is by vision'. ...And that the Lord's Community is the vehicle that transports the throne and the One seated upon it into all the Earth.

www.ingramcontent.com/pod-product-compliance
Lightning Source LLC
Chambersburg PA
CBHW071500040426
42444CB00008B/1421